Wildflowers
of Michigan
Field Guide

Stan Tekiela

Adventure Publications
Cambridge, Minnesota

Dedication

To my daughter, Abigail Rose. The sweetest flower in my life.

Acknowledgments

I would like to thank Kathy Heidel, a wonderful naturalist with extraordinary knowledge of the wildflowers of Michigan. I will always have a special place in my heart for her. And thanks to John D. Jackson, Ph.D., a botanist who continues to guide me through the wonderful world of wildflowers. Special thanks to naturalist Elise Martin Bushard and photographer Richard Haug for their help with this book.

Edited by Sandy Livoti

Cover, book design and illustrations by Jonathan Norberg

Cover photo: Wood Lily by **Stan Tekiela**

All photos copyright by **Stan Tekiela** unless otherwise noted.

Rick and Nora Bowers: 116; **Dudley Edmondson:** 8 (flat both, round both, spike left), 9 (bell right, composite both, irregular left, tube left), 10 (palmate left, twice compound both), 11 (alternate both, clasping right, opposite both, perfoliate left, whorl both), 18, 22, 28, 50 (inset), 82, 96, 102, 112, 170, 174, 180, 184 (both), 190, 194, 196, 218, 234, 242, 244, 248, 250, 254 (main), 266, 282, 288, 292, 302, 314, 328, 348, 350, 374, 394, 410; **Richard Haug:** 106, 110, 130, 142, 176, 200, 230, 246 (main), 260 (fruit), 278, 290, 340, 346; **Don Mammoser:** 220 (fruit); and **Larry Weber:** 98 (main), 126

10 9 8 7 6 5 4 3

Wildflowers of Michigan Field Guide
First Edition 2000, Second Edition 2021
Copyright © 2000 and 2021 by Stan Tekiela
Published by Adventure Publications
An imprint of AdventureKEEN
310 Garfield Street South
Cambridge, Minnesota 55008
(800) 678-7006
www.adventurepublications.net

All rights reserved
Printed in China

ISBN 978-1-64755-100-1 (pbk.); ISBN 978-1-64755-101-8 (ebook)

TABLE OF CONTENTS

Introduction

Sample Pages

The Wildflowers

Checklist/Index by Species

Glossary

Notes

About the Author

MICHIGAN AND WILDFLOWERS

Michigan is a great place for wildflower enthusiasts! Our state is at the crossroads of three major vegetative habitats. Each of these vegetative zones contains a wide and often unique variety of wildflowers. Our upper Midwest location is unique because we have a western wildflower influence, an even stronger eastern influence and a strong northern boreal influence. All of this means Michigan is fortunate to have an extremely diverse, often unique and certainly a very healthy variety of wonderful wildflowers.

The *Wildflowers of Michigan Field Guide* is an easy-to-use field guide to help the curious nature seeker identify 200 of the most common wildflowers in Michigan. It features, with only a few exceptions, the herbaceous wildflowers of Michigan. Herbaceous plants have soft green stems and die back to the ground each fall. Only a few plants with woody stems have been included because these particular plants are very common and have large showy flowers.

STRATEGIES FOR IDENTIFYING WILDFLOWERS

Determining the color of the flower is the first step in a simple five-step process to identify a wildflower.

Because this guide is organized by color, identifying an unknown wildflower is as simple as matching the color of the flower to the color section of the book. The color tabs on each page identify the color section.

The second step in determining the identity of a wildflower is the size. Within each color section, the flowers are arranged by the size of the flower, or flower cluster, from small to large. A plant with a single, small, yellow flower will be in the beginning of the yellow section while a large white flower will be towards the end of the white section. Sometimes flowers are made up of many individual flowers in clusters that are perceived to be one larger flower. Therefore, these will be ordered by the size of the cluster, not the individual flower. See page 432 for rulers to help estimate flower and leaf size.

Once you have determined the color and approximate size, observe the appearance of the flower. Is it a single flower or cluster of flowers? If it is a cluster, is the general shape of the cluster flat, round or spike? For the single flowers, note if the flower has a regular, irregular, bell or tube shape. Also, counting the number of petals might help to identify these individual flowers. Compare your findings with the descriptions on each page. Examining the flower as described above should result in narrowing the identity of the wildflower down to just a few candidates.

The fourth step is to look at the leaves. There are several possible shapes or types of leaves. Simple leaves have only one leaf blade but can be lobed. Compound leaves have a long central leaf stalk with many smaller leaflets attached. Twice compound leaves have two or more leaf stalks and many leaflets. Sometimes it is helpful to note if the leaves have toothed or smooth margins (edges), so look for this also.

For the fifth step, check to see how the leaf is attached to the stem. Some plants may look similar but have different leaf attachments so this can be very helpful. Look to see if the leaves are attached opposite of each other along the stem, alternately, or whorled around a point on the stem. Sometimes the leaves occur at the base of the plant (basal). Some leaves do not have a leaf stalk and clasp the stem at their base (clasping) and in some cases the stem appears to pass through the base of the leaf (perfoliate).

Using these five steps (color, size, shape, leaves and leaf attachment) will help you gather the clues needed to quickly and easily identify the common wildflowers of Michigan.

USING THE ICONS

Sometimes the botanical terms for leaf type, attachment and type of flower can be confusing and difficult to remember. Because of this, we have included icons at the bottom of each page. They can be used to quickly and visually match the main features of the plant to the specimen you are viewing without even needing to completely understand the botanical terms. By using the photos, text descriptions and icons in this field guide, you should be able to quickly and easily identify most of the common wildflowers of Michigan.

The icons are arranged from left to right in the following order: flower cluster type, flower type, leaf type, leaf attachment and fruit. The first two flower icons refer to cluster type and flower type. While these are not botanically separate categories, we have made separate icons for them to simplify identification.

Flower Cluster Icons

      (icon color is dependent on flower color)

Flat   Round   Spike

Any cluster (tightly formed group) of flowers can be categorized into one of three cluster types based on its over-all shape. The flat, round and spike types refer to the cluster shape which is easy to observe. Technically there is another cluster type, composite, which appears as a single daisy-like flower but is actually a cluster of many tiny flowers. Because this is often perceived as a flower type, we have included the icon in the flower type section. See page 9 for its description.

Some examples of cluster types

Flat   **Round**   **Spike**

Flower Type Icons

Regular **Irregular** **Bell** **Tube** **Composite**

(icon color is dependent on flower color)

Botanically speaking, there are many types of flowers but in this guide, we are simplifying them to five basic types. Regular flowers are defined as having a round shape with three or more petals, lacking a disk-like center. Irregular flowers are not round but uniquely shaped with fused petals. Bell flowers are hanging with fused petals. Tube flowers are longer and narrower than bell flowers and point up. Composite flowers (technically a flower cluster) are usually round compact clusters of tiny flowers appearing as one larger flower.

Some examples of flower types

Regular **Irregular** **Bell**

disk flowers
ray flowers

Tube **Composite**

Composite cluster: Although a composite flower is technically a type of flower cluster, we are including the icon in the flower type category since most people not familiar with botany would visually see it as a flower type, not a flower cluster. A composite flower consists of petals (ray flowers) and/or a round disk-like center (disk flowers). Sometimes a flower has only ray flowers, sometimes only disk flowers or both.

Leaf Type Icons

| Simple | Simple Lobed | Compound | Twice Compound | Palmate |

Leaf type can be broken down into two main types; simple and compound. Simple leaves are leaves that are in one piece; the leaf is not divided into smaller leaflets. It can have teeth or be smooth along the edges. The simple leaf is depicted by the simple leaf icon. Simple leaves may have lobes and sinuses that give the leaf a unique shape. These simple leaves with lobes are depicted by the simple lobed icon.

Some examples of leaf types

Simple   **Simple Lobed**   **Compound**

Twice Compound   **Palmate**

Compound leaves have two or more distinct, small leaves called leaflets that arise from a single stalk. In this field guide we are dividing compound leaves into regular compound, twice compound or palmately compound leaves. Twice compound leaves are those that have many distinct leaflets arising from a secondary leaf stalk. Palmately compound leaves are those with three or more leaflets arising from a common central point.

Leaf Attachment Icons

Alternate   **Opposite**   **Whorl**   **Clasping**   **Perfoliate**   **Basal**

Leaves attach to the stems in different ways. There are six main types of attachment, but a plant can have two different types of attachments. This is most often seen in the combination of basal leaves and leaves that attach along the main stem either alternate or opposite (cauline leaves). These wildflowers have some leaves at the base of the plant, usually in a rosette pattern, and some leaves along the stem. In these cases, both icons are included; for most plants, there will only be one leaf attachment icon.

Some examples of leaf attachment

Alternate   Opposite   Whorl

Clasping   Perfoliate   Basal

Alternate leaves attach to the stem in an alternating pattern while opposite leaves attach to the stem directly opposite from each other. Whorled leaves have three or more leaves that attach around the stem at the same point. Clasping leaves have no stalk and the base of the leaf partly surrounds the main stem. Perfoliate leaves are also stalkless and have a leaf base that completely surrounds the main stem. Basal leaves are those that originate at the base of a plant, near the ground, usually grouped in a round rosette.

Fruit Icons

     (icon color is dependent on berry or pod color)

Berry   Pod

In some flower descriptions a fruit category has been included. This may be especially useful when a plant is not in bloom or when the fruit is particularly large or otherwise noteworthy. Botanically speaking, there are many types of fruit. We have simplified these often confusing fruit categories into two general groups, berry and pod.

Some examples of fruit types

Berry   **Pod**

The berry icon is used to depict a soft, fleshy, often round structure containing seeds. The pod icon is used to represent a dry structure that, when mature, splits open to release seeds.

BLOOMING SEASON

Most wildflowers have a specific season of blooming. For example, you probably won't see the common spring-blooming Yellow Trout Lily blooming in summer or fall. Knowing the season of bloom can help you narrow your selection as you try to identify an unknown flower. In this field guide, spring usually means April, May and the first half of June. Summer refers to the last half of June, July and August. Fall usually means September and October.

LIFE CYCLE/ORIGIN

The life cycle of a wildflower describes how long a wildflower lives. Annual wildflowers are short-lived. They sprout, grow and bloom in only one season, never to return except from seed. Most wildflowers have perennial life cycles that last many years. Perennial wildflowers are usually deeply rooted plants that grow from the roots each year. They return each year from their roots, but they also produce seeds to start other perennial plants. Similar to the annual life cycle is the biennial cycle. This group of plants takes two seasons of growth to bloom. The first year the plant produces a low growth of basal leaves. During the second year, the plant sends up a flower stalk from which it produces seeds, from which new plants can be started. However, the original plant will not return for a third year of growth.

Origin indicates whether the plants are native or non-native. Most of the wildflowers in this book originate in Michigan and are considered native plants. Non-native plants were often unintentionally introduced when they escaped from gardens or farms. Most non-native plants are now naturalized in Michigan.

Some plants are also considered invasive (nonnative and capable of destructive spread) or noxious (detrimental to the environment, people or economy). Learn more about the problem plants and other invasives in Michigan by visiting www.michigan.gov/invasives.

HABITATS

Some wildflowers thrive only in specific habitats. They may require certain types of soil, moisture, pH levels, fungi or nutrients. Other wildflowers are generalists and can grow just about anywhere. Sometimes noting the habitat surrounding the flower in question can be a clue to its identity.

RANGE

The wide variety of habitats in Michigan naturally restricts the range of certain wildflowers that have specific requirements. For example, a wildflower such as Pearly Everlasting that requires dry acid soils may only be found in northeastern Michigan. Sometimes this section can help you eliminate a wildflower from consideration just based on its range. However, please keep in mind that the ranges indicated are general notations on where the flower is commonly found. They are general guidelines only and there will certainly be exceptions to these ranges.

STAN'S NOTES

Stan's Notes is fun and fact-filled with many interesting "gee-whiz" tidbits of information such as historical uses, other common names, insect relationship, color variations and much more. Much of the information in this section cannot be found in other wildflower field guides.

CAUTION

A word of caution. In Stan's Notes, it is mentioned that in some cultures, some of the wildflowers were used for medicine or food. While some find this interesting, DO NOT use this guide to identify edible or medicinal plants. Some of the wildflowers in Michigan are toxic or have toxic look-alikes that can cause severe problems. Do not take the chance of making a mistake. Please enjoy the wildflowers with your eyes, nose or with your camera. In addition, please don't pick, trample or transplant any of the wildflowers you see. The flower of a plant is its reproductive structure and if you pick a flower you have eliminated its ability to reproduce itself. Transplanting wildflowers is another destructive occurrence. Most wildflowers need specific soil types, pH levels or special bacteria or fungi in the soil to grow properly. If you try to transplant a wildflower to a habitat not suitable for its particular needs, the wildflower most likely will die. Many of our Michigan wildflowers are now available from your local garden centers. These wildflowers have been cultivated and have not been dug from the wild.

Enjoy the Wild Wildflowers!

Common Name
Scientific name

Color Indicator —

Family: plant family name

Height: average range of mature plant

Flower: general description, type of flower, size of flower, number of petals

Leaf: general description, size, leaf type, type of attachment, toothed or smooth

Fruit: berry or pod

Bloom: spring, summer, fall

Cycle/Origin: annual, perennial, biennial, native, non–native

Habitat: general environment in which you are likely to find the flower

Range: an approximate range where the flower is found

Stan's Notes: helpful identification information, history, origin and other interesting, "gee-whiz" nature facts

Not all icons are found on every page. See preceding pages for icon descriptions.

CLUSTER TYPE
Spike

FLOWER TYPE
Irregular

LEAF TYPE
Palmate

LEAF ATTACHMENT
Basal

FRUIT
Pod

Forget-me-not
Myosotis scorpioides

Family: Borage (Boraginaceae)

Height: 6–12" (15–30 cm)

Flower: a fusion of 5 petals forms tiny baby blue flowers with yellow centers (eye); each flower, ¼" (.6 cm) wide, sits atop 2 uncoiling stems; stems are curled and unfurl when the flowers begin to bloom

Leaf: blunt, lance-shaped stemless leaves, 1–2" (2.5–5 cm) long, alternate along the stem; each leaf is covered in fine hair

Bloom: spring, summer, fall

Cycle/Origin: perennial, non-native

Habitat: wet, shade, along streams, rivers and creeks

Range: locally around cities and homes

Stan's Notes: Also called True Forget-me-not, this Eurasian import has escaped gardens and grows along Michigan's rivers and streams. It can live directly in water but is usually found in moist soil, growing in large mats along an extensive fibrous root system. Seven species of Forget-me-not are found in Michigan; only two are native. Another old name for this plant, Scorpion Weed, refers to its coiled flower stalk, which resembles the coiled tail of a scorpion. Some suggest that the common name comes from the plant's unpleasant taste or odor that is hard to forget. Another story is about a suitor who reached too far over a cliff to obtain the flower for his love, fell and cried out, "Forget me not!"

FLOWER TYPE **Regular**   LEAF TYPE **Simple**   LEAF ATTACHMENT **Alternate**

19

Creeping Charlie
Glechoma hederacea

Family: Mint (Lamiaceae)

Height: 5–8" (12.5–20 cm)

Flower: light blue-to-purple flowers, ¼–¾" (.6–2 cm) long; 2–4 flowers on short stalks that arise at a leaf joint; 5 petals fuse to form a flower

Leaf: round, sometimes kidney-shaped leaves, ½–1½" (1–4 cm) wide, with deep veins and coarse scalloped teeth along the edge; often purplish in color with a wavy edge

Bloom: spring, summer

Cycle/Origin: perennial, non-native

Habitat: dry, shade, disturbed soil and especially lawns

Range: throughout

Stan's Notes: This is not an ivy, but a Eurasian import of the Mint family. Like all mints, its stem is square and it has opposite leaves. It roots to the ground at each leaf attachment (node), allowing the plant to creep across the ground, hence one of its common names, Ground Ivy. Another common name, Gill-over-the-ground, comes from the French *guiller*, or "to ferment," because its leaves were once used to ferment and flavor beer. It grows in large carpets in moist semi-shaded areas and is considered a weed because of its aggressive growing nature.

FLOWER TYPE   LEAF TYPE   LEAF ATTACHMENT
Irregular   **Simple**   **Opposite**

Blue-eyed Grass
Sisyrinchium montanum

Family: Iris (Iridaceae)

Height: 4–20" (10–50 cm)

Flower: a collection of tiny blue flowers with a bright yellow center, individual flowers, ½" (1 cm) wide, have 6 petals, each tipped with a small point; each flower group rises from a short stalk, which in turn comes from a longer leaflike stem

Leaf: thin, pointed, grass-like leaves, ¼" (.6 cm) wide, up to 20" (50 cm) long, that are often confused with blades of grass

Fruit: a round pod

Bloom: spring, summer

Cycle/Origin: perennial, native

Habitat: wet, meadows, roadsides, prairies

Range: northern half of the L.P. and throughout the U.P.

Stan's Notes: Often confused with a type of grass, Blue-eyed Grass is actually a member of the Iris family. The most common of several species in Michigan and one of over 40 species in North America, Blue-eyed Grass has fibrous vertical roots, unlike the more common irises, which spread on a horizontal rhizome. Like other irises, Blue-eyed Grass is made up of three sepals (leaves that look like petals) and three petals. Each petal is shallowly notched with tiny tips. Stems can sometimes be bluish purple.

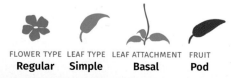

FLOWER TYPE	LEAF TYPE	LEAF ATTACHMENT	FRUIT
Regular	**Simple**	**Basal**	**Pod**

Round-lobed Hepatica
Anemone americana

Family: Buttercup (Ranunculaceae)

Height: 4–6" (10–15 cm)

Flower: flowers have 5–9 petal-like sepals that range in color from pale blue to lavender, pink and white, and have 3 green bracts underneath; each flower, ½–1" (1–2.5 cm) wide, sits on a single hairy stalk that may droop

Leaf: each basal leaf has 3 round lobes rising from a thin hairy stalk

Bloom: spring

Cycle/Origin: perennial, native

Habitat: dry, shade, deciduous woods

Range: throughout

Stan's Notes: One of the spring ephemerals, the Round-lobed Hepatica retains its leaves all winter and quickly sends up flowers each spring before the trees above have a chance to produce leaves and shade it out. Previous year's leaves are dark purple to brown, while new growth is a light green. Called "Hepatica" because the lobes of the leaves resemble the three lobes of the liver, which early herbalists interpreted to mean that this plant was good for treatment of liver troubles—not true. Also called Liverleaf. Nearly identical to Sharp-lobed Hepatica (pg. 27), which has pointed lobed leaves. The stems of pollinated flowers lengthen and droop toward the ground, where ants collect and disperse the seeds.

FLOWER TYPE
Regular

LEAF TYPE
Simple Lobed

LEAF ATTACHMENT
Basal

Sharp-lobed Hepatica
Anemone acutiloba

Family: Buttercup (Ranunculaceae)

Height: 4–6" (10–15 cm)

Flower: flowers have 5–9 petal-like sepals that range in color from pale blue to white, lavender and pink, and have 3 green bracts underneath; each flower, ½–1" (1–2.5 cm) wide, sits on a single hairy stalk that may droop

Leaf: each basal leaf has 3 sharply pointed lobes rising from a thin hairy stalk

Bloom: spring

Cycle/Origin: perennial, native

Habitat: dry, shade, deciduous woods

Range: throughout, but more common in the L.P.

Stan's Notes: Nearly identical to Round-lobed Hepatica (pg. 25) with the exception of the shape of the leaf. The dark purple-to-brown leaves from last season remain under snow and become active when snow melts, allowing the plant to "awake" earlier than other woodland plants. New green leaves are produced shortly after. The name "Hepatica" refers to the three lobes of the leaves that resemble the three lobes on the human liver, which is why early herbalists believed this plant was good for the treatment of liver disease. Flowers stand on tall erect stems but lengthen after pollination and droop to the forest floor where ants can reach the forming seeds, which they collect and disperse.

FLOWER TYPE
Regular

LEAF TYPE
Simple Lobed

LEAF ATTACHMENT
Basal

Harebell
Campanula rotundifolia

Family: Bellflower (Campanulaceae)

Height: 6–20" (15–50 cm)

Flower: pale blue-to-purple bell-shaped flowers, ¾" (2 cm) long, each formed from 5 fused petals and found nodding from a thin stem

Leaf: round basal leaves, ½–1" (1–2.5 cm) wide, that often wither before flowering, and linear grass-like leaves, 3" (7.5 cm) long and ⅛–¼" (.3–.6 cm) wide, alternate along the stem

Bloom: summer

Cycle/Origin: perennial, native

Habitat: wet, sun, rocky outcroppings along rivers, meadows, prairies

Range: throughout

Stan's Notes: Also called Bluebell, Harebell, one of nine species of *Campanula* found in Michigan, is the smallest member with the thinnest and weakest stem. Its basal leaves are round, hence the species name, *rotundifolia*, or "round leaf." Like other members of this genus, its stems exude a milky sap. Its drooping flowers are adapted for specific insect pollination and also protect the pollen from rain and dew. The Harebell often grows in clumps and does well in gardens, but please don't dig it from the wild. This circumpolar plant grows at similar latitudes all around the world.

FLOWER TYPE	LEAF TYPE	LEAF ATTACHMENT	LEAF ATTACHMENT
Bell	**Simple**	**Alternate**	**Basal**

Asiatic Dayflower
Commelina communis

Family: Spiderwort (Commelinaceae)

Height: 1–3' (30–90 cm)

Flower: usually only one blue-and-white flower, ¾" (2 cm) wide, located at the tip of each stem; flower has 3 petals—2 upper blue and 1 lower white

Leaf: toothless, stalkless, lance-shaped leaves, 3–5" (7.5–12.5 cm) long, attach directly to the stem, with the leaf base folding around the stem at the point of attachment; leaves nearest the flowers are much smaller and nearly heart-shaped, sometimes cradling the flower

Bloom: spring, summer, fall

Growth: annual, non-native

Habitat: moist, disturbed areas, roadsides, gardens

Range: in and around large metropolitan areas of the state

Stan's Notes: As its name suggests, the Asiatic Dayflower, essentially a garden weed, was introduced from Asia. It is usually found only in metro areas because it most often reaches gardens from purchased bags of soil. Flowers bloom only for one day, hence the common name, "Dayflower." Its species name, *communis*, refers to the colonies it forms by rooting from each stem node (where each leaf attaches). Only two species of dayflower are found in Michigan. This is a host plant for Pearl Crescent butterfly caterpillars.

FLOWER TYPE
Irregular

LEAF TYPE
Simple

LEAF ATTACHMENT
Alternate

LEAF ATTACHMENT
Clasping

Large-leaved Aster
Eurybia macrophylla

Family: Aster (Asteraceae)

Height: 1–5' (30–150 cm)

Flower: delicate, pale blue (sometimes white) flowers, 1" (2.5 cm) wide, each with 10–20 petals (ray flowers) and a yellow center (disk flowers) that turns red with age; 2–20 flowers per plant grow on a purplish-colored stem

Leaf: large, coarsely toothed, heart-shaped basal leaves, soft to touch, 4–8" (10–20 cm) long, that are deeply notched where they attach to the stalk; smaller, stalkless, lance-shaped leaves alternate along the stem (cauline)

Bloom: summer, fall

Cycle/Origin: perennial, native

Habitat: dry, shade, deciduous woods

Range: throughout

Stan's Notes: A very common plant of northern Michigan, the Large-leaved Aster sometimes carpets the ground, excluding other plants. Only about 1 in 50 plants sends up a flower stalk each year. The plant reproduces along a horizontal underground root system (rhizomes). Its flower stalks are sticky to the touch because of miniature glands. Because of their size and availability, the large leaves of this plant are often used as emergency toilet paper.

FLOWER TYPE
Composite

LEAF TYPE
Simple

LEAF ATTACHMENT
Alternate

LEAF ATTACHMENT
Basal

Tall Bellflower

Campanula americana

Family: Bellflower (Campanulaceae)

Height: 3–6' (90–180 cm)

Flower: a single spike cluster, 1–2' (30–60 cm) long; individual flowers, 1" (2.5 cm) wide, are light blue-to-purple with a white ring in the center of the flower (throat); each flower is made up of 5 pointed (and often twisted) petals

Leaf: pointed, toothed lance-shaped leaves, 3–6" (7.5–15 cm) long

Bloom: summer

Cycle/Origin: perennial, native

Habitat: wet, shade, deciduous woods, along forest edges

Range: southern half of the L.P.

Stan's Notes: A tall native flower of the shady borders of deciduous woods, Tall Bellflower is one of the tallest members of the Bellflower family, often growing to 5–6' (150–180 cm). Its regular flowers are unusual because most members of this family have tube or bell-like flowers. Bellflower is a biennial that re-seeds itself. In its first year, it's a tight rosette of leaves; in its second year, it sends up a flower stalk.

CLUSTER TYPE	FLOWER TYPE	LEAF TYPE	LEAF ATTACHMENT
Spike	**Regular**	**Simple**	**Alternate**

35

Common Blue Violet
Viola sororia

Family: Violet (Violaceae)

Height: 4–10" (10–25 cm)

Flower: unusual, deep bluish lavender or white flowers, 1" (2.5 cm), each with 5 distinct petals; center of flower white with the 3 lower petals strongly veined; flowers usually below the leaves and found on their own stalk

Leaf: characteristically heart-shaped leaves, scalloped tooth with surface of leaf often woolly and rolled along the edge; each leaf rises from the base of the plant on its own woolly stalk

Fruit: ¼" green pod that turns brown

Bloom: spring

Cycle/Origin: perennial, native

Habitat: wet or moist woodland, gardens and disturbed soils

Range: throughout

Stan's Notes: Almost 80 distinct species in North America and over 900 worldwide. Looks very similar to other blue violets. Many botanists have now lumped together many species of violets under one species name, *V. sororia*. Like all violets, the flowers appear highly variable in color. Closely related to a common annual, the pansy (not shown). Often pops up in shady gardens and in lawns. Reproduces mostly by underground runners, but produces a seed pod with many tiny brown seeds. Leaves are high in vitamins and have been used in salads or cooked greens.

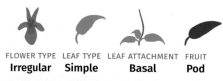

FLOWER TYPE	LEAF TYPE	LEAF ATTACHMENT	FRUIT
Irregular	**Simple**	**Basal**	**Pod**

Bottle Gentian
Gentiana andrewsii

Family: Gentian (Gentianaceae)

Height: 1–2' (30–60 cm)

Flower: a round, dense cluster of bluish purple closed-tube flowers, 1–1½" (2.5–4 cm) long, sits atop the plant; each flower is made up of 5 fused petals that provide no apparent entrance into the flower

Leaf: toothless, lance-shaped leaves with 3 main veins; their sides bend upwards to form a trough; opposite leaves lower and whorled leaves near each flower cluster

Fruit: papery pod, roughly the size and shape of the flowers, contains hundreds of tiny brown seeds

Bloom: summer, fall

Cycle/Origin: perennial, native

Habitat: moist, sun, prairies, along railroad beds, old fields

Range: throughout the L.P. and scattered in the U.P.

Stan's Notes: The Bottle Gentian is also called the Closed Gentian due to its curiously closed flowers, which keep out all but the largest insects. Bumblebees force themselves inside the flower through the top by pushing apart the petals. A wonderful perennial of the prairie, also called Prairie Gentian, this wildflower can also be grown in a garden—but please do not dig it from the wild. One of at least six species of gentian in Michigan.

FLOWER TYPE	LEAF TYPE	LEAF ATTACHMENT	LEAF ATTACHMENT	FRUIT
Tube	**Simple**	**Opposite**	**Whorl**	**Pod**

Virginia Waterleaf
Hydrophyllum virginianum

Family: Waterleaf (Hydrophyllaceae)

Height: 1–2' (30–60 cm)

Flower: round cluster, 1–1½" (2.5–4 cm) wide, of light blue-to-white, bell-shaped flowers, each ¼–½" (.6–1 cm) long; each flower has 5 petals that fuse to form a bell, and its inner flower parts conspicuously stick out beyond the petals

Leaf: large leaves, 5–6" (12.5–15 cm) long, with 5–7 sharply toothed lobes per leaf; leaves are often covered in white or gray "water spots"

Bloom: spring

Cycle/Origin: perennial, native

Habitat: moist deciduous woods

Range: southern half of the L.P.

Stan's Notes: A common plant of moist deciduous forests, Virginia Waterleaf often grows in large mats by reproducing along underground roots (rhizomes). Its leaves are often covered with white "water spots," hence the common name, "Waterleaf." The leaf spots are more obvious early in the spring and fade by early summer; the entire plant dies back to the ground by midsummer. A shade-loving plant that works well as ground cover or as fill-in for a shady yard or garden. Use a hand lens to view the center of the flower. The frilly stamens form a beautiful lavender pink lace.

CLUSTER TYPE
Round

FLOWER TYPE
Bell

LEAF TYPE
Simple Lobed

LEAF ATTACHMENT
Alternate

Creeping Bellflower
Campanula rapunculoides

Family: Bellflower (Campanulaceae)

Height: 1–3' (30–90 cm)

Flower: soft bluish purple, bell-shaped flowers, 1–2" (2.5–5 cm) long, line up along a tall stem and almost always point downward; each flower is comprised of 5 sharply pointed petals fused together to form the bell-shaped flower

Leaf: heart-shaped lower leaves, 2" (5 cm) long, lance-shaped stem leaves (cauline) with fine teeth, ½–1" (1–2.5 cm) long

Fruit: downward-drooping pod-like containers hold many tiny seeds

Bloom: summer, fall

Growth: perennial, non-native

Habitat: dry, sun, fields, old homesteads

Range: throughout

Stan's Notes: Although native to Eurasia, the Creeping Bellflower is also called the European Bellflower and was undoubtedly introduced to the U.S. through Europe. Once a common garden plant, it has escaped cultivation and can now be found growing in the wild near old homesteads and abandoned gardens. It flowers only on one side of the stem. Spreads by underground stems, and once established, it is often difficult to eliminate.

FLOWER TYPE	LEAF TYPE	LEAF ATTACHMENT	FRUIT
Bell	**Simple**	**Alternate**	**Pod**

Spiderwort
Tradescantia occidentalis

Family: Spiderwort (Commelinaceae)

Height: 10–24" (25–60 cm)

Flower: a cluster of up to 10 flowers, each 1–2" (2.5–5 cm) wide, with 3 violet-blue petals surrounding a golden yellow center; flowers open only a few at a time and are sometimes pink to white

Leaf: grass-like leaves, 15" (37.5 cm) long, clasp the stem; each leaf is folded lengthwise, forming a V-groove

Bloom: spring, summer

Cycle/Origin: perennial, native

Habitat: dry, sandy ridges, meadows, fields, along roads

Range: southern half of the L.P.

Stan's Notes: An unusual-looking plant with exotic-looking flowers. Flowers open in the morning and often wilt by noon on hot days. The common name "Spider" comes from several unique characteristics. One is the angular leaf attachment suggestive of the legs of a sitting spider, or the stringy, mucilaginous sap that strings out like a spider's web when the leaf is torn apart. The name "wort" means "plant." The genus name *Tradescantia* is in honor of J. Tradescant, an English gardener.

FLOWER TYPE
Regular

LEAF TYPE
Simple

LEAF ATTACHMENT
Alternate

LEAF ATTACHMENT
Clasping

45

Heal-all
Prunella vulgaris

Family: Mint (Lamiaceae)

Height: 6–12" (15–30 cm)

Flower: thick compact spikes, 1–2" (2.5–5 cm) long, of violet-blue flowers; individual flowers, ½" (1 cm) long, have upper petals forming a hood, while lower petals form a landing platform (lip) for insects

Leaf: lance-shaped toothless leaves, 1–3" (2.5–7.5 cm) long, with short leafstalks; leaves sometimes have tiny wing-like leaves, ⅓" (.8 cm) long, growing from the point of attachment

Bloom: spring, summer, fall

Cycle/Origin: perennial, non-native

Habitat: wet, shade, lawns, fields, along roads

Range: throughout

Stan's Notes: Also called Self-heal and All-heal. The common names refer to this plant's use as a folk medicine in many cultures throughout the world. It is most commonly used in throat remedies, but little evidence of its effectiveness exists. Heal-all grows in large patches in lawns (where it prefers light shade) and will adapt to being mowed, forming a very low plant 2" (5 cm) tall. Like most members of the Mint family, Heal-all has a square stem and opposing leaves and emits a faint odor when crushed.

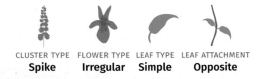

CLUSTER TYPE	FLOWER TYPE	LEAF TYPE	LEAF ATTACHMENT
Spike	**Irregular**	**Simple**	**Opposite**

Teasel
Dipsacus fullonum

Family: Teasel (Dipsacaceae)

Height: 2–6' (60–180 cm)

Flower: many tiny lavender-blue-to-white flowers, ½"
(1 cm) long, tightly arranged in a round cluster
on an egg-shaped head, 1–3" (2.5–7.5 cm) tall;
long pointed bracts at base of flowering head

Leaf: leaves, 4–16" (10–40 cm) long; toothed with the
upper leaves fused together at the stem (perfoliate)

Bloom: summer, fall

Cycle/Origin: biennial, non-native

Habitat: roadsides, old fields, disturbed soils

Range: throughout

Stan's Notes: A tall plant with thistle-like spines on the stem. The
flower heads dry nicely, lasting well into winter, and are sometimes used in dried flower arrangements. A non-native plant that
was brought from Europe. The dried heads were cultivated by
wool companies, fixed as spindles and used to raise the nap or
tease the wool cloth, hence the common name. There are over
250 species of teasel and all are native to the Old World.

CLUSTER TYPE **Round** FLOWER TYPE **Tube** LEAF TYPE **Simple** LEAF ATTACHMENT **Opposite** LEAF ATTACHMENT **Perfoliate**

Chicory
Cichorium intybus

Family: Aster (Asteraceae)

Height: 1–4' (30–120 cm)

Flower: sky blue stalkless flowers, 1½" (4 cm) wide, each with up to 20 petals (ray flowers) sparsely populate a tall stem and close by early afternoon; petals are square-tipped and fringed; the color ranges from white to pink, depending upon age and location

Leaf: long, toothed basal leaves similar to those of a dandelion, 3–6" (7.5–15 cm) long; stem leaves (cauline) are oblong and much smaller, ½–1" (1–2.5 cm) long, lack teeth and clasp the stem

Bloom: summer, fall

Cycle/Origin: perennial, non-native

Habitat: dry, sun, along roads, open fields

Range: throughout

Stan's Notes: Also called Blue Sailor or Ragged Sailor. Chicory's few flowers open one at a time and last only one day. This European import, believed to come from Eurasia, was brought to the U.S. to be cultivated for its long taproot, which can be roasted and ground as a coffee substitute or additive. Its leaves, like those of the dandelion, are edible, high in vitamins and minerals, but quite bitter.

FLOWER TYPE
Composite

LEAF TYPE
Simple

LEAF ATTACHMENT
Alternate

LEAF ATTACHMENT
Basal

LEAF ATTACHMENT
Clasping

Fringed Gentian
Gentianopsis crinita

Family: Gentian (Gentianaceae)

Height: 1–3' (30–90 cm)

Flower: deep violet-blue flowers, 2" (5 cm) long, 1 per stalk, with blue-tipped green sepals surrounding 4 elongated petals that form the flower tube; each petal is frayed or fringed on the end

Leaf: lance-shaped toothless leaves, 1–2" (2.5–5 cm) long, with a round base nearly clasp the stem; prominent central vein ends at a pointed tip

Bloom: summer, fall

Cycle/Origin: biennial, native

Habitat: wet, prairies, meadows, along streams

Range: throughout the L.P.

Stan's Notes: A spectacular flower of prairies, Fringed Gentian is a true biennial that takes two years to bloom and should never be picked or dug. One of the last wildflowers to bloom, it waits until late summer or autumn to produce flowers. Its ragged petal tips provide the first part of its common name, "Fringed." The second part, "Gentian," comes from King Gentius of Illyria, who discovered some medicinal properties in its roots. The Fringed Gentian is often found growing in wet spots within native prairies. The flower relies on a mycorrhizal relationship, the lack of which directly affects the presence or abundance of this wildflower.

FLOWER TYPE
Tube

LEAF TYPE
Simple

LEAF ATTACHMENT
Opposite

53

Wild Blue Phlox
Phlox divaricata

Family: Phlox (Polemoniaceae)

Height: 10–20" (25–50 cm)

Flower: round clusters, 2–3" (5–7.5 cm) wide, of pale blue flowers; individual flowers, 1" (2.5 cm) wide, are made up of 5 petals fused together at the base into a short tube

Leaf: toothless, lance-shaped leaves, 1–2" (2.5–5 cm) long, grow opposite along the stem without a leafstalk

Bloom: spring, summer

Cycle/Origin: perennial, native

Habitat: wet, shade, deciduous woods

Range: throughout the L.P.

Stan's Notes: Also called Wood Phlox or Blue Phlox, Wild Blue Phlox is a single-stemmed woodland wildflower that grows in the dappled sunlight of the forest floor. Its fragrant flowers are occasionally white or dark blue, and its stems are often hairy and sticky to the touch. It is closely related to garden phlox. Closed flower buds have twisted petals appearing like a torch; the name "Phlox" is Greek for "flame." This plant blooms around Mother's Day and in bygone years was often picked to add to wildflower bouquets for Mother.

CLUSTER TYPE	FLOWER TYPE	LEAF TYPE	LEAF ATTACHMENT
Round	**Regular**	**Simple**	**Opposite**

Blue Vervain
Verbena hastata

Family: Vervain (Verbenaceae)

Height: 2–6' (60–180 cm)

Flower: tall thin spikes, 2–5" (5–12.5 cm) long, of small, deep blue-to-purple, tube-like flowers, ⅛" (.3 cm) long; 5 petals fuse at the base to form a short tube

Leaf: matched pairs of narrow, lance-shaped, toothed leaves, 4–6" (10–15 cm) long; lower leaves are sometimes 3-lobed

Bloom: summer

Cycle/Origin: perennial, native

Habitat: wet, along ditches, shores, wet fields, roadsides

Range: throughout

Stan's Notes: Blue Vervain is a tall slender plant with multiple pencil-thin flower spikes that bloom from the bottom up. Its stems are square with opposite leaves, which is why it is often confused with a member of the Mint family. In ancient times, it was thought the plant had medicinal properties, giving rise to the genus name *Verbena*, Latin for "sacred plant." It rarely produces a pink flower and is often confused with Hoary Vervain (pg. 161). Visited by many butterflies and bees for its high nectar content.

CLUSTER TYPE	FLOWER TYPE	LEAF TYPE	LEAF ATTACHMENT
Spike	**Regular**	**Simple**	**Opposite**

Blue Flag Iris

Iris versicolor

Family: Iris (Iridaceae)

Height: 2–3' (60–90 cm)

Flower: several large blue or violet flowers, 2½–4" (6–10 cm) wide, rising on tall stiff stalks; the center of the lowest petals (sepals) are beardless (no bristles) with a white patch (throat) trimmed in yellow

Leaf: narrow grass-like blades, 1" (2.5 cm) wide and 8–32" (20–80 cm) long; similar to garden irises

Fruit: large green pod, 1½–2" (4–5 cm) long, with round ends containing multiple seeds

Bloom: spring, summer

Cycle/Origin: perennial, native

Habitat: wet, sun or shade, edges of wetlands, lakes and rivers

Range: northern half of the L.P. and the entire U.P.

Stan's Notes: Also called Northern Iris, this wildflower is usually found along water, growing in clumps of tall, erect, sword-like leaves with many flowers. These clumps are created by toxic, horizontal underground roots (rhizomes), which many cultures have used as medicine. Its largest petals are actually modified leaves (sepals). Insects entering the flower must walk along the sepals and pass under the plant's male and female flower parts, thus completing pollination. "Iris" is derived from the Greek word for "rainbow," and describes the wide range of flower colors in the Iris family.

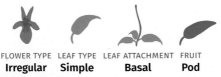

FLOWER TYPE	LEAF TYPE	LEAF ATTACHMENT	FRUIT
Irregular	**Simple**	**Basal**	**Pod**

Wild Lupine
Lupinus perennis

Family: Pea or Bean (Fabaceae)

Height: 1–3' (30–90 cm)

Flower: a spike, 3–7" (7.5–18 cm) long, of blue pea-like flowers, each ⅔" (1.6 cm) wide; what appear to be 3 petals (called, from the top down, standard, wing and keel) are actually 5 petals fused together

Leaf: leaf stems arise from base of the plant and end with a palmate leaf, 5–10" (12.5–25 cm) wide, made of 7–11 small leaflets

Fruit: initially many green, fuzzy, pea-pod-shaped fruits, up to 2" (5 cm) long, turn black when mature, contain 10–20 small brown-to-black seeds

Bloom: late spring, early summer

Cycle/Origin: perennial, native

Habitat: dry, sandy soils in open woods, mostly in sunny fields or along roads, prairies

Range: southeastern half of the L.P.

Stan's Notes: These pea-like flowers open under the weight of an insect, revealing horn-shaped stamens that deposit pollen on the visitor. This is the only host plant for the Karner Blue butterfly caterpillar, a threatened species in Michigan. A closely related garden escapee (*L. polyphyllus*) has multicolored flowers and grows in dense clusters (see inset photo).

CLUSTER TYPE	FLOWER TYPE	LEAF TYPE	LEAF ATTACHMENT	FRUIT
Spike	**Irregular**	**Palmate**	**Basal**	**Pod**

Pickerelweed
Pontederia cordata

Family: Pickerelweed (Pontederiaceae)

Height: aquatic

Flower: many spike clusters, 4–6" (10–15 cm) long, of blue flowers; individual flowers, ½" (1 cm) long, have 3 upper petals (the middle upper petal has 2 small yellow spots) and 3 lower petals

Leaf: pointed, toothless, heart-shaped leaves, 4–10" (10–25 cm) long, rise from an underwater root; each leaf is indented at the base, where the stalk attaches

Bloom: summer

Cycle/Origin: perennial, native

Habitat: lakes, wetlands, ponds, streams

Range: throughout

Stan's Notes: An aquatic plant that forms large mats, the Pickerelweed's leaves and flowers rise above the water (it is rooted to the bottom of lakes). The common name refers to the Pickerel, a fish that shares a similar watery habitat. Leaves are similar to Arrowhead (pg. 215), but the flowers are completely different in color, size and shape. It prefers shallow water, unlike the deep-water-loving White Water Lily (pg. 321) and the Yellow Water Lily (pg. 405). Visited by a small solitary bee, *Dufourea novaeangliae*, which visits only this plant for nectar and pollen.

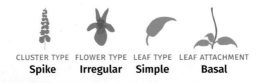

CLUSTER TYPE **Spike** FLOWER TYPE **Irregular** LEAF TYPE **Simple** LEAF ATTACHMENT **Basal**

Wild Ginger
Asarum canadense

Family: Birthwort (Aristolochiaceae)

Height: 6–12" (15–30 cm)

Flower: a single, brown-to-greenish red, tube-shaped flower, 1–2" (2.5–5 cm) long, with 3 pointed lobes; located between 2 leafstalks at ground level

Leaf: a pair of large heart–shaped leaves, 3–6" (7.5–15 cm) wide; each leaf is soft and velvety due to dense hairs and has a deep notch where the stalk attaches

Bloom: spring

Cycle/Origin: perennial, native

Habitat: moist, shade, deciduous woods

Range: throughout

Stan's Notes: Wild Ginger's large flowers are located at ground level to accommodate ground-dwelling insects, such as beetles, that pollinate its flower. Its stems and leaves are covered with long white hairs, and each plant has a single flower located between the pair of leafstalks. It grows from a long horizontal rootstock and has a strong ginger-like odor when crushed (it is not, however, the same species of ginger that is used in Asian cooking).

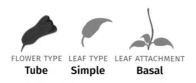

FLOWER TYPE
Tube

LEAF TYPE
Simple

LEAF ATTACHMENT
Basal

Skunk Cabbage
Symplocarpus foetidus

Family: Arum (Araceae)

Height: 1–2' (30–60 cm)

Flower: brown-to-purple shell-like covering (spathe), 3–6" (7.5–15 cm) tall, often mottled with spots of green, encloses an off-white or yellow club-like spike (spadix) that is covered with many tiny flowers

Leaf: large, bright green leaves, deeply veined, on very short stalks that are often unseen, rising from the base of the flower

Bloom: early spring

Cycle/Origin: perennial, native

Habitat: wet or moist woodland, along streams and wetlands

Range: throughout, mostly in southern half of the L.P.

Stan's Notes: One of the earliest plants to bloom each spring. Highly unusual flower that grows so rapidly that its cellular respiration produces enough heat to actually melt any snow or ice around it. The flowers have a strong odor of dead or decaying flesh that attracts early flying insects, such as flesh flies, that mistake the flower as carrion and inadvertently pollinate the flowers. Closely related to Jack-in-the-pulpit (pg. 81). Exceptionally large leaves appear after the flowers and grow up to 2' (60 cm) tall and up to 1' (30 cm) wide. Leaves also smell of dead flesh when crushed.

CLUSTER TYPE **Spike**   LEAF TYPE **Simple**   LEAF ATTACHMENT **Basal**

Pineapple-weed
Matricaria discoidea

Family: Aster (Asteraceae)

Height: 3–8" (7.5–20 cm)

Flower: several (often many) small, green-to-yellow dome-shaped flowers, ¼" (.6 cm) tall

Leaf: individual leaves highly divided into thin, parsley-like leaves, ½–1" (1–2.5 cm) long

Bloom: summer, fall

Cycle/Origin: annual, native

Habitat: dry, sun, along roads, disturbed soils, farmyards

Range: throughout

Stan's Notes: A small inconspicuous plant that grows in disturbed soils along sidewalks, roads and gardens, the Pineapple-weed is so named because its flowers and leaves smell strongly of pineapple when crushed. It also makes a delicious yellow tea. A type of aster, it has a composite flower only of disk flowers, lacking petals (ray flowers). A close relative to Wild Chamomile (not shown), which has white daisy-like petals (ray flowers).

FLOWER TYPE
Composite

LEAF TYPE
Simple Lobed

LEAF ATTACHMENT
Alternate

69

fruit

Smooth Solomon's Seal
Polygonatum biflorum

Family: Asparagus (Asparagaceae)

Height: 1–3' (30–90 cm)

Flower: groups of 2–10, green, 6-petaled, bell-shaped flowers, ½–1" (1–2.5 cm) long, hang from short stalks, 1" (2.5 cm) long; flower stalks arise from a leaf base (axis)

Leaf: toothless, lance-shaped, stalkless leaves, 2–6" (5–15 cm) long, clasp an arching stem; conspicuous parallel veining makes the leaf look light green

Fruit: blue-to-black berries, ¼" (.6 cm) round

Bloom: spring

Cycle/Origin: perennial, native

Habitat: dry, shade, deciduous woods

Range: southern half of the L.P.

Stan's Notes: Also called True Solomon's Seal, this plant is distinguished by its long arching stems that grow up to 3' (90 cm) long. To remember the difference between True and False Solomon's Seal (pg. 319), use this rhyme: "Solomon's Seal, to be real, must have flowers along its keel." Although the species name suggests two flowers, (*bi* means "two"; *florum* means "flower") it can grow up to ten flowers per leaf axis. The plant grows from a large underground rootstock (rhizome). When its stalk breaks away, it leaves a distinctive round mark resembling the seal of King Solomon. Native Americans once gathered its roots for food, but the roots may leave one's mouth tingling and numb.

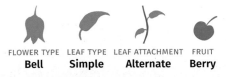

FLOWER TYPE	LEAF TYPE	LEAF ATTACHMENT	FRUIT
Bell	**Simple**	**Alternate**	**Berry**

Wild Sarsaparilla
Aralia nudicaulis

Family: Ginseng (Araliaceae)

Height: 1–2' (30–60 cm)

Flower: 3 distinct round clusters, 1–2" (2.5–5 cm) wide, made of greenish white flowers; individual flowers, ¼" (.6 cm) long, have 5 tiny white petals

Leaf: 2 main stalks, each of which spreads into 3 leaf-stalks that grow 3–5 fine-toothed oval leaflets, 3–4" (7.5–10 cm) long, with pointed ends

Fruit: clusters of round purple-to-black berries, ⅛" (.3 cm), on a leafless stalk

Bloom: spring, summer

Cycle/Origin: perennial, native

Habitat: dry, shade, coniferous woods, deciduous woods

Range: throughout

Stan's Notes: A perennial of coniferous and deciduous woodland, just about every part of the Wild Sarsaparilla comes in threes, including its leaf stems, leaflets and flower stalks. Its horizontal underground roots are very aromatic and have been used as a substitute for sarsaparilla in root beer. Its clusters of purple-to-black berries are eaten by wildlife, and its leaves usually rise well above the flowers, often concealing them. The species name *nudicaulis* comes from the Latin *nudus* for "naked" and *cauli* for "stalk," and refers to the plant's leafless flower stalk.

CLUSTER TYPE
Round

FLOWER TYPE
Regular

LEAF TYPE
Compound

LEAF ATTACHMENT
Basal

FRUIT
Berry

fruit

Blue Cohosh

Caulophyllum thalictroides

Family: Barberry (Berberidaceae)

Height: 1–3' (30–90 cm)

Flower: a round cluster, 2" (5 cm) wide, of up to 20 greenish yellow flowers; individual flowers, ½" (1 cm) wide, have 6 pointed, petal-like sepals surrounding 6 smaller rounded petals

Leaf: a leaf is divided into several stalks and as many as 27 small leaflets; each leaflet, 1–3" (2.5–7.5 cm) long, has 3–5 pointed lobes; in spring, leaves and stems are often purplish blue in color

Fruit: dark blue berry on a thick stalk

Bloom: spring

Cycle/Origin: perennial, native

Habitat: wet, deciduous woods, shade

Range: throughout

Stan's Notes: A shade-loving plant of the deciduous forest, Blue Cohosh flowers range in color from greenish yellow to purplish brown. An erect, single main stem, purplish blue in color in spring, is covered with a light dusting of white powder that is easily wiped off. The poisonous blue berries sit atop a characteristically thickened stem and together they resemble a miniature light bulb. The leaves resemble those of Early Meadow Rue (pg. 79) or Tall Meadow Rue (pg. 315), hence the species name, *thalictroides*.

CLUSTER TYPE	FLOWER TYPE	LEAF TYPE	LEAF ATTACHMENT	FRUIT
Round	**Regular**	**Compound**	**Alternate**	**Berry**

Ragweed
Ambrosia trifida

Family: Aster (Asteraceae)

Height: 2–10' (60–300 cm)

Flower: spike cluster, 1–5" (2.5–12.5 cm) long, of tiny green flowers, ⅛" (.3 cm) wide; cluster on short stem arising from leaf axis

Leaf: lobed leaf, 3–8" (7.5–20 cm) long, with 3 narrow pointed lobes, sharp teeth; the leafstalk has long white hairs

Bloom: summer, fall

Cycle/Origin: annual, native

Habitat: roadsides, fields, disturbed soils

Range: throughout

Stan's Notes: Also known as Giant Ragweed, Kingweed or Tall Ambrosia, it has become more common over the past 200 years, coinciding with agricultural expansion in North America. Very tall plants with inconspicuous green flowers that produce thousands of seeds eaten by many bird species. The green flowers don't attract insects for pollination. The pollen is instead spread by wind and consequently is a principal cause of hay fever each summer and fall.

CLUSTER TYPE
Spike

LEAF TYPE
Simple Lobed

LEAF ATTACHMENT
Alternate

Early Meadow Rue
Thalictrum dioicum

Family: Buttercup (Ranunculaceae)

Height: 1–3' (30–90 cm)

Flower: a loose, open, round cluster, 2–3" (5–7.5 cm) wide, of whitish green hanging flowers; individual flowers, ¼" (.6 cm) wide, are made up of 4–5 petal-like sepals with showy, thread-like, yellow hanging flower parts (stamens)

Leaf: bluish green leaves that characteristically droop; each leaflet, ½" (1 cm) long, has 3 tooth-like lobes

Fruit: a single ribbed, egg-shaped, pod-like container, ⅛" (.3 cm) long

Bloom: spring

Cycle/Origin: perennial, native

Habitat: wet, shade, moist woods

Range: mostly in lower half of the L.P.

Stan's Notes: Sometimes a very difficult species to identify correctly, Early Meadow Rue is a shorter version of the Tall Meadow Rue (pg. 315). It grows in moist or wet depressions within woodlands, and has dark red-to-purple stems and droopy leaves. Male and female flowers grow on different plants, hence the species name, *dioicum*, which is Greek for "two houses" or "two plants." Its flowers are wind pollinated, but are also visited by bees, butterflies and other insects. Often associated with Sugar Maple and Basswood trees.

CLUSTER TYPE
Round

FLOWER TYPE
Bell

LEAF TYPE
Twice Compound

LEAF ATTACHMENT
Alternate

FRUIT
Pod

79

fruit

Jack-in-the-pulpit
Arisaema triphyllum

Family: Arum (Araceae)

Height: 1–3' (30–90 cm)

Flower: an erect club (spadix or "Jack"), 2–3" (5–7.5 cm) long, sits inside a green or purplish hood (spathe or "pulpit") at the top of a single stalk; base of the green club is lined with tiny separate male or female flowers, protected by the hood

Leaf: 1 or 2 (female plant has 2; male has 1) large, dull green, deep-veined, compound leaves, 5–12" (12.5–30 cm) long, made up of 3 leaflets

Fruit: cluster of shiny green berries that turn red in autumn

Bloom: spring

Cycle/Origin: perennial, native

Habitat: wet, shade, moist deciduous woods

Range: throughout

Stan's Notes: Also called Indian Turnip because Native Americans cooked its short, thickened, underground stem (corm) as food. However, no part of the plant is considered edible as it contains calcium oxalate crystals, which cause a burning sensation in the mouth. Its large three-part leaves are often confused with Large-flowered Trillium (pg. 309) leaves, but Jack-in-the-pulpit has a deep vein that runs around the leaf's entire margin. If disturbed or affected by other stress, the female plant declines in vigor and may stop producing fruit.

CLUSTER TYPE	LEAF TYPE	LEAF ATTACHMENT	FRUIT
Spike	**Compound**	**Alternate**	**Berry**

81

Alumroot

Heuchera richardsonii

Family: Saxifrage (Saxifragaceae)

Height: 2–3' (60–90 cm)

Flower: a spike cluster, 2–4" (5–10 cm) tall, of green-to-brown bell flowers, ¼" (.6 cm) wide, on a tall, thin leafless flower stalk; 5 petals form each bell-shaped flower

Leaf: maple-leaf-shaped basal leaves, 3–4" (7.5–10 cm) wide; hairy stalks; each leaf is coarsely toothed, hairy beneath, and made up of 3–5 lobes

Bloom: spring, summer

Cycle/Origin: perennial, native

Habitat: dry, prairies, along roads, fields, open woods, rock outcroppings

Range: southern half of the L.P.

Stan's Notes: Alumroot grows in a wide variety of habitats, from prairies to woodlands to rock outcroppings. Its thick root was used as an astringent in folk medicine, hence the common name, Alum. The genus name *Heuchera* is in honor of Johann von Heucher, an eighteenth-century German physician and botanist. A similar species (*H. americana*) grows in shaded woodlands. A member of the Saxifrage family, the name comes from two Latin words that mean "rock" and "break," referring to its habit of growing in rock outcroppings.

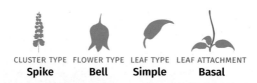

CLUSTER TYPE	FLOWER TYPE	LEAF TYPE	LEAF ATTACHMENT
Spike	**Bell**	**Simple**	**Basal**

Orange Hawkweed
Hieracium aurantiacum

Family: Aster (Asteraceae)

Height: 1–2' (30–60 cm)

Flower: 2–10 bright orange flower heads, ¾–1" (2–2.5 cm) wide, made up of 20–30 individual ray flowers, grow on a single stem; only a few open at a time

Leaf: simple, linear, toothless and stalkless, hair-covered leaves, 2–5" (5–12.5 cm) long, with rounded ends

Bloom: summer

Cycle/Origin: perennial, non-native

Habitat: dry, sun, fields, disturbed soils, pastures, along roads

Range: throughout

Stan's Notes: Also known as King-devil or Devil's Paintbrush, as its single stem is topped with a red-orange color, resembling a painter's brush. This plant originated in Eurasia as an alpine plant. Now naturalized in North America, it is sometimes considered a noxious weed. It grows in large patches, spreading by aboveground runners. This single-stemmed plant will hold up to ten flower heads that close at night and on cloudy days. After pollination, its flowering heads produce a dandelion-like silk to carry away its seeds. The name "Hawkweed" came from the mistaken belief that hawks ate the flowers to improve their vision. Fifteen species of hawkweed grow in Michigan, and it is often mistaken for an orange daisy.

FLOWER TYPE **Composite**　LEAF TYPE **Simple**　LEAF ATTACHMENT **Basal**

85

fruit

Spotted Touch-me-not

Impatiens capensis

Family: Touch-me-not (Balsaminaceae)

Height: 3–5' (90–150 cm)

Flower: orange flowers, 1" (2.5 cm) long, covered with reddish brown spots; each flower has a large open mouth that leads to a long, thin, sharp-curved tube (spur)

Leaf: sharp-toothed, oval leaves, 1–3" (2.5–7.5 cm) long, alternate on short leafstalks, 1" (2.5 cm)

Fruit: thin, banana-shaped pod-like containers

Bloom: summer

Cycle/Origin: annual, native

Habitat: wet, shade, wetlands, along streams

Range: throughout

Stan's Notes: Also called Jewelweed because water droplets on its leaves shine like tiny jewels, the Spotted Touch-me-not is a tall annual plant of wet areas. Its stems are nearly translucent and contain a slippery juice that can be used to soothe the sting from nettles or Poison Ivy. Its long, thin, ripe seed pods explode when touched, throwing seeds in all directions. This action, combined with the dark spots on its flowers, provide the common name. A similar species, Jewelweed (*I. pallida*), also known as Pale Touch-me-not (pg. 357), has yellow flowers that are not as spotted. Scrape off the ripe seed's dark brown covering to discover a sky blue nutlet inside. An important nectar plant for hummingbirds.

FLOWER TYPE
Tube

LEAF TYPE
Simple

LEAF ATTACHMENT
Alternate

FRUIT
Pod

87

Wood Lily
Lilium philadelphicum

Family: Lily (Liliaceae)

Height: 2–3' (60–90 cm)

Flower: large, upright, reddish orange flowers, 2–3" (5–7.5 cm) wide, with 6 petals (actually 3 petals and 3 sepals), all covered with dark purplish spots on a faint yellow background; 1 to 8 flowers per plant

Leaf: a whorl of 4–7 narrow, lance-shaped leaves, 2–3" (5–7.5 cm) long

Fruit: oblong pod, 2" (5 cm) long

Bloom: summer

Cycle/Origin: perennial, native

Habitat: wet, sun, prairies, dry deciduous and coniferous woods

Range: throughout

Stan's Notes: A showy perennial lily of the woodland habitats, the Wood Lily is the only upright pointing lily. It is also called Prairie Lily because it grows in prairies of western states. It grows from a large, scaly underground bulb. Wood Lily is toxic to cats if ingested and shouldn't be grow in gardens visited by domestic cats. Also called Fire Lily, Western Red Lily, or Philadelphia Lily.

FLOWER TYPE **Regular**   LEAF TYPE **Simple**   LEAF ATTACHMENT **Whorl**   FRUIT **Pod**

Michigan Lily
Lilium michiganense

Family: Lily (Liliaceae)

Height: 3–7' (90–210 cm)

Flower: large, dangling, orange-to-yellow flowers, 2–3" (5–7–5 cm) wide, with 6 backward-curving petals (actually 3 petals and 3 sepals), all covered with dark purplish spots and yellow centers that fade to orange; 1 to 8 flowers per plant

Leaf: a whorl of 4–6 narrow, lance-shaped leaves, 2–6" (5–15 cm) long

Fruit: oblong pod, 2" (5 cm) long

Bloom: summer

Cycle/Origin: perennial, native

Habitat: wet, sun, along roads in wet ditches, moist woods

Range: southern half of the L.P. and scattered in the western U.P.

Stan's Notes: Also called Turk's-cap Lily because of the curled flower petals resembling a Turkish hat. Once common along country roads, it has decreased due to the mowing and draining of ditches. A big showy lily that grows from a large, scaly underground bulb, it can grow up to 20 flowers per plant. Native Americans once gathered its bulbs for food.

FLOWER TYPE **Regular**   LEAF TYPE **Simple**   LEAF ATTACHMENT **Whorl**   FRUIT **Pod**

fruit

Butterfly-weed
Asclepias tuberosa

Family: Dogbane (Apocynaceae)

Height: 1–2' (30–60 cm)

Flower: a large, flat-topped cluster, 2–3" (5–7.5 cm) wide, made of small, individual orange flowers, ⅜" (.9 cm) wide, each with downward-curved petals

Leaf: hairy toothless leaves, 2–6" (5–15 cm) long, widen at tip

Fruit: erect small clusters of narrow pods, 6" (15 cm) long, covered in fine hairs; pods contain large brown seeds with silken "parachutes" to carry away each seed

Bloom: spring, summer

Cycle/Origin: perennial, native

Habitat: dry, sun, prairies, prefers sandy soils

Range: throughout the L.P.

Stan's Notes: Found in prairies and along railroad beds growing in clumps, this true milkweed lacks milky sap; instead, its stem and leaves bleed clear sap. The species name *tuberosa* refers to its large taproot, which makes it nearly impossible to transplant (it can be grown from seed). Its single stems branch only near the top and its flower stalks harbor up to 25 individual flowers. Its flowers vary from all yellow to red, and its roots and stems have been used in folk medicine. A host plant for Gray Hairstreak and Monarch butterfly caterpillars.

CLUSTER TYPE **Flat**   FLOWER TYPE **Irregular**   LEAF TYPE **Simple**   LEAF ATTACHMENT **Alternate**   FRUIT **Pod**

Four-o'clock
Mirabilis nyctaginea

Family: Four-o'clock (Nyctaginaceae)

Height: 1–3' (30–90 cm)

Flower: pink or purple flowers, ¼–½" (.6–1 cm) wide, made up of 5 notched petals fused together at the base; small clusters of flowers are set against a green shield called a bract

Leaf: pairs of heart-shaped leaves, 2–4" (5–10 cm) long, opposite on the stem

Bloom: spring, summer, fall

Cycle/Origin: annual or perennial, depending on location, native

Habitat: wet or dry, sun or shade, woodlands or disturbed soils, highly adaptive plant

Range: throughout the L.P. and scattered in the U.P.

Stan's Notes: A single-stemmed plant that branches only near the top into flower stalks, its flowers open late in the afternoon (hence the common name) and last until the following day, usually wilting by noon. Blooming overnight suggests that it might be pollinated by night-flying insects, such as moths. Its stems are four-sided and smooth, and it often grows along roads or in disturbed soils and gardens. Four species of four-o'clock can be found in Michigan. In southern Michigan, this plant is a perennial. In northern Michigan where the climate is harsher, it grows only as an annual. Visited by Sphinx Moths (also known as Hummingbird Moths) for its nectar.

FLOWER TYPE **Regular**   LEAF TYPE **Simple**   LEAF ATTACHMENT **Opposite**

Pointed-leaved Tick-trefoil

Desmodium glutinosum

Family: Pea or Bean (Fabaceae)

Height: 1–4' (30–120 cm)

Flower: spike cluster, 5–14" (12.5–36 cm) long, of up to 12–15 pink flowers, ¼–1" (.6–2.5 cm) long, that are sparsely spaced on a single hairy stem

Leaf: compound leaves, 5–7" (12.5–18 cm) long, with 3 pointed leaflets, 2–3" (5–7.5 cm) long; 2 side (lateral) leaflets are on short leafstalks, ¼" (.6 cm) long; sharply pointed end (terminal) leaflet is on a longer leafstalk, 1–2" (2.5–5 cm) long; up to 4 compound leaves arising from a single whorl of stalks

Fruit: triangular-shaped brown pods are covered with hooked hairs

Bloom: summer

Cycle/Origin: perennial, native

Habitat: dry woodland

Range: throughout

Stan's Notes: This common forest floor plant might go unnoticed until its triangular seeds covered with hooked hairs stick to your pants and socks. Grows with a single stem in which all leafstalks emanate from a central whorl. Terminal leaflets have characteristically long stalks and pointed tip. Usually found growing under mature maples, elms and oaks. Birds and wildlife eat seeds.

CLUSTER TYPE
Spike

FLOWER TYPE
Irregular

LEAF TYPE
Compound

LEAF ATTACHMENT
Whorl

FRUIT
Pod

fruit

Rose Twisted-stalk
Streptopus lanceolatus

Family: Lily (Liliaceae)

Height: 1–3' (30–90 cm)

Flower: pink, bell-shaped flowers, ⅓" (.8 cm) long, with 6 petals hang on crooked, thread-like stalks from the main stem of the plant at each leaf joint (axil)

Leaf: lance-shaped leaves 2–3" (2.5–5 cm) long, with obvious parallel veins clasp the stem; edge of leaf (margin) fringed with minute hairs

Fruit: round red berry

Bloom: spring, summer

Cycle/Origin: perennial, native

Habitat: moist deciduous woods

Range: northern one-third of the LP and the entire UP

Stan's Notes: A single arching stemmed plant of moist woodland. The pink bell flowers produce bright red berries. Look for the characteristic twisted or zigzag stem. A single leaf attaches at each turn of the stem. The stem and the edges of the leaves are covered with minute hairs. The genus name breaks down to *streptos* and *pous*, which are Greek for "twisted" and "foot" or "stalk," hence its common name. The berries are mildly cathartic (cause diarrhea), so don't eat them.

FLOWER TYPE
Bell

LEAF TYPE
Simple

LEAF ATTACHMENT
Alternate

LEAF ATTACHMENT
Clasping

FRUIT
Berry

99

Spreading Dogbane
Apocynum androsaemifolium

Family: Dogbane (Apocynaceae)

Height: 1–4' (30–120 cm)

Flower: groups of 2–10 tiny, pink-to-white, bell-shaped flowers, ⅓" (.8 cm) long; individual flowers are white with pink stripes; 5 petals fuse together to form the bell

Leaf: simple, oval, toothless leaves, 2–4" (5–10 cm) long, often with a wavy edge

Fruit: long thin pods, 3–8" (7.5–20 cm), that open along 1 side, revealing seeds attached to long tufts of white fuzz

Bloom: summer

Cycle/Origin: perennial, native

Habitat: dry, sun, along roads, edges of deciduous woods

Range: throughout

Stan's Notes: A tall perennial plant with a single main stem that branches out into many "spreading" stems. A close relative of the milkweeds, it produces a thick, white, milky juice in its stem and leaves; this juice contains cardiac glycosides that cause hot flashes, rapid heartbeat and fatigue. Insects avoid this plant because of the poisonous juice. When dried and peeled, the stem makes a strong cord. Once used by Native Americans for fishing and trapping. The same fibers are selectively used by orioles as nest-building material.

FLOWER TYPE	LEAF TYPE	LEAF ATTACHMENT	FRUIT
Bell	**Simple**	**Opposite**	**Pod**

Twinflower
Linnaea borealis

Family: Honeysuckle (Linnaeaceae)

Height: 3–6" (7.5–15 cm)

Flower: a pair of small, pink, bell flowers, ½" (1 cm) long, each with 5 petals fused to form a bell; flowers hang from a single, thinly-forked stem

Leaf: small, round, toothless, evergreen leaves, ½" (1 cm) wide, paired low on the stem; leaves are light green and shiny

Bloom: summer

Cycle/Origin: perennial, native

Habitat: coniferous woods, bogs, rock outcroppings

Range: throughout

Stan's Notes: A low-growing evergreen plant, Twinflower forms patches by trailing stems along the ground and sending up short, thin flower stalks with a pair of leaves near the base and a pair or "twin set" of fragrant pink flowers. This common flower is found in northern coniferous forests throughout the world (circumpolar). The genus name *Linnaea* honors the father of botany, C. Linnaeus (1707–1778), who developed the modern way of naming plants and animals by using two names of usually Latin, but sometimes Greek, derivation—genus and species.

FLOWER TYPE	LEAF TYPE	LEAF ATTACHMENT
Bell	**Simple**	**Opposite**

103

Spring Beauty

Claytonia virginica

Family: Miner's Lettuce (Montiaceae)

Height: 6–10" (15–25 cm)

Flower: showy, upright flowers, ½–¾" (1–2 cm) wide, whitish with pink veining; each flower is made up of 5 petals with a slightly yellow-tinted center

Leaf: usually a single pair of oppositely attached grass-like leaves, 2–4" (5–10 cm) long, located about midway up the stem

Bloom: spring

Cycle/Origin: perennial, native

Habitat: wet, shade, deciduous woods, clearings in woods

Range: southern half of the L.P.

Stan's Notes: Spring Beauty often grows in large patches, reproducing from small, underground, potato-like tubers. The flower's pink veins act as signposts or runways to guide insects to the nectar. As they "taxi in," the insects brush against stamens, loading up on pollen, then off to another flower where they drop a few grains on the receptive stigma. This plant's numbers have been reduced because of the over-gathering of these tubers for food, so please don't dig them up. One of many in the Miner's Lettuce family, a group of about 230 species of plants worldwide, Spring Beauty is a very attractive flower that flowers early in spring, hence its common name. A variety can be purchased at your local garden center to grow in your garden.

FLOWER TYPE   LEAF TYPE   LEAF ATTACHMENT
Regular   **Simple**   **Opposite**

Wild Mint
Mentha arvensis

Family: Mint (Lamiaceae)

Height: 6–24" (15–60 cm)

Flower: open round cluster, 1" (2.5 cm) wide, of tiny pale lilac-pink or white flowers, ¼" (.6 cm) long, clustered around the square stem at each leaf axis

Leaf: pairs of lance-shaped leaves, 1–2" (2.5–5 cm) long, tapering at both ends, opposite on the stem; leaves get smaller near the top of the plant; strong odor when crushed

Bloom: summer, fall

Cycle/Origin: perennial, native

Habitat: wet woodland, along streams and lakes

Range: throughout

Stan's Notes: One of the common mints in Michigan. Because plants have no way of eliminating waste, they store by-product chemicals in their leaves in the form of essential oils. The oils, which give the leaves of this plant a minty smell and taste, have been used as flavoring in beverages and other foods. In the genus of the so-called "true mints." The tiny flowers have four lobes, referred to as lips.

CLUSTER TYPE **Round**   FLOWER TYPE **Irregular**   LEAF TYPE **Simple**   LEAF ATTACHMENT **Opposite**

Crown Vetch
Securigera varia

Family: Pea or Bean (Fabaceae)

Height: 1–2' (30–60 cm); climbing vine

Flower: round clusters, 1" (2.5 cm) wide, of pink-and-white flowers; individual flowers ¼–½" (.6–1 cm) wide, are pea-like with pink upper petals (standard) and white side petals (wings)

Leaf: each leaf, 2–4" (5–10 cm) long, is made up of 12–25 round leaflets, ½–¾" (1–2 cm) wide

Fruit: flat pea-like pod, 1–2" (2.5–5 cm) long

Bloom: summer

Cycle/Origin: perennial, non-native

Habitat: dry, sun, along roads, open fields

Range: throughout the L.P.

Stan's Notes: A plant introduced from Eurasia and North Africa, the Crown Vetch was first planted here to stop erosion along roads after construction. It grows in very large masses, 25–35' (7.6–10.7 m) across, by stems that creep across the ground. When in flower, the large patches bloom into an impressive display of pink-and-white flowers. Once planted, the Crown Vetch is hard to remove. Like most members of the Pea or Bean family, Crown Vetch can fix nitrogen from the air into the soil, thus improving soil fertility.

CLUSTER TYPE
Round

FLOWER TYPE
Irregular

LEAF TYPE
Compound

LEAF ATTACHMENT
Alternate

FRUIT
Pod

Pipsissewa
Chimaphila umbellata

Family: Heather (Ericaceae)

Height: 6–12" (15–30 cm)

Flower: a round cluster, 1–2" (2.5–5 cm) wide, of 3–7 waxy pink-to-white flowers; individual flowers, ½" (1 cm) wide, have 5 pointed petals; flowers sometimes hang down

Leaf: 2 or 3 tiers of whorled, shiny evergreen leaves, each whorl has 4–6 leaves; leaves are 1–3" (2.5–7.5 cm) long, with sharp teeth on the upper wider portion of the leaf

Bloom: summer

Cycle/Origin: perennial, native

Habitat: dry, shade, coniferous woods

Range: throughout

Stan's Notes: A small single-stemmed plant with whorled evergreen leaves, typically found growing under pine trees. The upper portion of the flower stalk is reddish pink, matching the color of the flowers. The genus name, *Chimaphila*, is from the Greek words *cheima* (winter) and *philein* (to love), which describes the evergreen leaves. The species name, *umbellata*, describes the umbrella-shaped flower cluster.

CLUSTER TYPE
Round

FLOWER TYPE
Regular

LEAF TYPE
Simple

LEAF ATTACHMENT
Whorl

Common Valerian
Valeriana officinalis

Family: Valerian (Valerianaceae)

Height: 2–3' (60–90 cm)

Flower: a compact round cluster, 1–3" (2.5–7.5 cm) wide, of flowers grows at the top of a single stem; individual flowers, white to light pink, ¼" (.6 cm) wide, are made up of 5 petals

Leaf: opposite pairs of deeply divided, fern-like leaves, 1–3" (2.5–7.5 cm) long; each leaf has many (11–21) narrow segments

Bloom: spring, summer

Cycle/Origin: perennial, non-native

Habitat: wet or dry, sun, along roads, old gardens, fields

Range: isolated in and around major cities

Stan's Notes: A native of Eurasia, Common Valerian was originally planted in gardens, but has escaped and is now naturalized in and around Michigan's major cities. This plant has been used medicinally for many centuries. Its roots contain valeric acid, a chemical that attracts domestic house cats. Also called Garden Heliotrope.

CLUSTER TYPE
Round

FLOWER TYPE
Regular

LEAF TYPE
Simple Lobed

LEAF ATTACHMENT
Opposite

fruit

seeds

Common Milkweed
Asclepias syriaca

Family: Dogbane (Apocynaceae)

Height: 2–5' (60–150 cm)

Flower: cream-colored, pink-tinged flowers, ½" (1 cm) wide, form a round cluster up to 2" (5 cm) wide; each flower has 5 downward-pointing petals and a 5-part pointed crown

Leaf: large, toothless, oval leaves, 4–6" (10–15 cm) long, bleed a white milky sap when broken

Fruit: elongated, green dry pods that split open to release many flat, brown seeds, each attached to hair-like fuzz that carries the seed on the wind

Bloom: summer

Cycle/Origin: perennial, native

Habitat: wet or dry, sun or shade, fields

Range: throughout

Stan's Notes: There are over 4,000 species in the dogbane/milk-weed family; just under 12 in Michigan. A unique pollination system involves sacs of pollen that snag on an insect's leg; the insect then unwittingly inserts the sacs into slits on other flowers. The plant's milky sap contains cardiac glycosides and, if eaten, will cause hot flashes, rapid heart rate and general weakness. The Monarch butterfly lays its eggs exclusively on milkweeds. Monarch caterpillars ingest the toxic sap with no ill effects, but they then become toxic to birds and other animals. Fibers from old stems are used by orioles for making nests.

CLUSTER TYPE	FLOWER TYPE	LEAF TYPE	LEAF ATTACHMENT	FRUIT
Round	**Irregular**	**Simple**	**Opposite**	**Pod**

Everlasting Pea
Lathyrus latifolius

Family: Pea or Bean (Fabaceae)

Height: 1–7' (30–210 cm)

Flower: spike cluster, 1–5" (2.5–12.5 cm) long, of pea-like pink flowers; cluster of 4–10 individual flowers, 1" (2.5 cm) wide, on elongated stems; flower color ranges from pink to blue to white

Leaf: 2 lance-shaped or elliptical leaflets, 1–3" (2.5–7.5 cm) long, on the end of a flat winged stalk; may have forked tendril from the tip of the leafstalk

Bloom: summer, fall

Cycle/Origin: perennial, non-native

Habitat: roadsides, fields, disturbed soils

Range: throughout

Stan's Notes: A weak-stemmed climbing vine that climbs up on other plants by taking hold with its forked tendrils. Stems are winged, like the leafstalks. Flowers are usually pink, but can be blue to white. Long flower stalk, up to 8 inches (20 cm) long, lacks the wings. Has two pair (four total) of narrow pointed stipules at the base of each leafstalk. Seeds are poisonous.

CLUSTER TYPE
Spike

FLOWER TYPE
Irregular

LEAF TYPE
Compound

LEAF ATTACHMENT
Alternate

117

Hedge Nettle

Stachys palustris

Family: Mint (Lamiaceae)

Height: 1–2' (30–60 cm)

Flower: a single spike cluster, 2–3" (5–7.5 cm) long, of irregular pink flowers; individual flowers, ½–1" (1–2.5 cm) wide, have a pink upper hood and 3-lobed lower petals with dark purple spots and veins

Leaf: opposite lance-shaped leaves, 3–6" (7.5–15 cm) long, covered with coarse teeth and a deep network of veins; little or no leafstalk

Bloom: summer

Cycle/Origin: perennial, native

Habitat: wet, sun, along small lakes and streams, wet meadows and prairies

Range: throughout

Stan's Notes: Like most members of the Mint family, Hedge Nettle has a square stem with opposite leaves, but unlike others, it lacks a fragrance. Its single stem is covered with woolly hair. The Hedge Nettle's common name comes from its growing habitat along the edge (or hedge) of wetlands, growing in the same habitat as the Stinging Nettle. It is also called Common Woundwort because it was once used to help heal all types of wounds.

CLUSTER TYPE	FLOWER TYPE	LEAF TYPE	LEAF ATTACHMENT
Spike	**Irregular**	**Simple**	**Opposite**

Showy Lady's Slipper
Cypripedium reginae

Family: Orchid (Orchidaceae)

Height: 1–3' (30–90 cm)

Flower: a spectacular flower, 2–3" (5–7.5 cm) tall, with 3 white, pointed, upper petal-like sepals and 1 large, inflated pink-and-white lower petal; the lower inflated petal is often veined in deep pink; hairy, flowering stalks

Leaf: basal leaves, 10" (25 cm) long and up to 2" (5 cm) wide, with deeply ribbed parallel veins, clasp the stem; leaves on flower stem are smaller, clasping, alternating

Fruit: elliptically shaped pod-like capsule, 2" (5 cm) long, containing extremely small seeds

Bloom: summer

Cycle/Origin: perennial, native

Habitat: wet, sun, swamps, slow-moving streams, moist woods

Range: throughout

Stan's Notes: The Showy Lady's Slipper is the largest and most impressive of the orchids found in the state. It should never be handled or dug, as this long-lived plant takes up to fifteen years to mature and form flowers. Some people get a Poison-Ivy-like rash from touching its stem's glandular hairs. Also called the Pink-and-white Lady's Slipper.

FLOWER TYPE
Irregular

LEAF TYPE
Simple

LEAF ATTACHMENT
Alternate

LEAF ATTACHMENT
Basal

FRUIT
Pod

Pink Lady's Slipper
Cypripedium acaule

Family: Orchid (Orchidaceae)

Height: 6–15" (15–37.5 cm)

Flower: a single large pink flower, 2½" (6 cm) tall, per each leafless stalk; flowers are made up of an inflated lower petal (slipper) with red veins and a groove down the middle, along with 3 pointed and twisted greenish brown sepals

Leaf: a pair of deep-veined basal leaves, up to 10" (25 cm) long, silvery beneath

Fruit: an erect pod-like container, 1–2" (2.5–5 cm) long

Bloom: spring, summer

Cyclo/Origin: perennial, native

Habitat: dry, shade, coniferous woods

Range: throughout

Stan's Notes: Also called Moccasin Flower, Pink Lady's Slipper is found growing in dry pine forests and sometimes among rocky outcroppings. One of the largest orchids in Michigan, it produces only one flower per stalk (rarely, a second flower). Its flower is usually a deep rosy red (sometimes white) that becomes pale with age. Small bees enter the flower through a slit running the length of the lower inflated petal. Once inside, the bee can't back out and proceeds to the other side, picking up a pollen sac, which can then be deposited in the next orchid. Do not attempt to transplant.

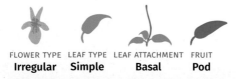

FLOWER TYPE	LEAF TYPE	LEAF ATTACHMENT	FRUIT
Irregular	**Simple**	**Basal**	**Pod**

Motherwort
Leonurus cardiaca

Family: Mint (Lamiaceae)

Height: 2–4' (60–120 cm)

Flower: spike clusters, 3–6" (7.5–15 cm) tall; individual flowers, pink-to-lilac and spine-tipped, ⅓" (.8 cm) long, arise near the stem at each leaf attachment (axil)

Leaf: sharp-toothed opposite leaves, 2–4" (5–10 cm) long, with 3 pointed lobes

Bloom: summer

Cycle/Origin: perennial, non-native

Habitat: wet or dry, sun or shade, fields, disturbed soils, gardens

Range: throughout

Stan's Notes: A common plant of forgotten backyards or abandoned gardens, Motherwort originated in Asia and was imported from Europe. Its long history of medicinal use included cultivation to treat heart ailments; hence its species name, *cardiaca* (heart). The common name, "Motherwort," refers to its traditional use as a menstrual disorder treatment. Like other members of the Mint family, it has a square stem and opposite leaves. To identify, look for its three distinctive sharp-lobed leaves; the lower leaves have three lobes, while the upper leaves only have three sharp points in place of lobes.

CLUSTER TYPE
Spike

FLOWER TYPE
Irregular

LEAF TYPE
Simple Lobed

LEAF ATTACHMENT
Opposite

Pink Pyrola

Pyrola asarifolia

Family: Heather (Ericaceae)

Height: 6–15" (15–37.5 cm)

Flower: a single, red-stemmed, spike cluster, 3–6" (7.5–15 cm) long, with up to 20 pink flowers; individual flowers, ¼–½" (.6–1 cm) wide, have 5 round petals; regular flowers, but often hang down to bell flowers

Leaf: round, dark green, evergreen basal leaves, 2–3" (5–7.5 cm) long, with red stalks

Fruit: a 5-chambered pod-like container

Bloom: summer

Cycle/Origin: perennial, native

Habitat: moist deciduous and coniferous woods

Range: throughout, except for the southeastern L.P.

Stan's Notes: A single, red-stemmed plant of moist woodlands, this is also called Shinleaf. There are five species of *Pyrola* in Michigan. This is the only one with a pink flower; the rest are white-flowered. The thick, dark green leaves are evergreen. There are no leaves on the flower stalk. All the *Pyrola* species contain an aspirin-like substance. The leaves were made into a leaf plaster and used to treat wounds and reduce pain. The leaf plaster was called Shinplaster, resulting in its other common name. Often grows in a large group.

CLUSTER TYPE	FLOWER TYPE	LEAF TYPE	LEAF ATTACHMENT	FRUIT
Spike	**Regular**	**Simple**	**Basal**	**Pod**

Pale Corydalis
Corydalis sempervirens

Family: Poppy (Papaveraceae)

Height: 6–24" (15–60 cm)

Flower: a spike cluster, 3–6" (7.5–15 cm) long, of dangling pink-and-yellow tubular flowers; individual flowers, ½" (1 cm) long, are made up of 4 petals which form the pink tube; ends of petals have an upturned yellow lip

Leaf: pale blue-green leaves, divided into many 3-lobed leaflets, ½" (1 cm) long

Fruit: thin, green pod-like container 1–2" (2.5–5 cm) long, turns brown when mature

Bloom: spring, summer

Cycle/Origin: perennial, native

Habitat: dry, sun, rock outcroppings

Range: throughout, except for the southeastern L.P.

Stan's Notes: A delicate herb of rocky outcroppings, Pale Corydalis is one of three species of *Corydalis* in Michigan. Its pale blue-green leaves and dangling pink-and-yellow flowers help to identify this plant. Later in summer, the flowers produce thin, green seed pods that turn brown and release seeds when mature. *Corydalis* is Greek for "crested lark," referring to the shape of the flowers.

CLUSTER TYPE
Spike

FLOWER TYPE
Tube

LEAF TYPE
Compound

LEAF ATTACHMENT
Alternate

FRUIT
Pod

Sweet Joe-pye Weed
Eutrochium purpureum

Family: Aster (Asteraceae)

Height: 2–7' (60–210 cm)

Flower: round cluster, 5–10" (12.5–25 cm) wide, of dull pinkish purple flower heads containing hundreds of small ¼" (.6 cm) composite (all disk) flowers; stem is green with small white hairs, often purplish at leaf joint

Leaf: whorls of 3–4 lance-shaped leaves, each 3–9" (7.5–22.5 cm) long, with a coarse-toothed edge; often smells of vanilla when crushed

Bloom: summer

Cycle/Origin: perennial, native

Habitat: dry, thickets, open woods

Range: southern half of the L.P.

Stan's Notes: A tall and robust plant that likes dry soil in woods or thickets. One of several similar species of Joe-pye in Michigan, it is often confused with Joe pye Weed (pg. 133), which has flat clusters of flowers and spots on its stem. Named after Joe Pye, a Native American medicine man. The flowers are very attractive to many species of butterflies. A good garden plant that can be purchased at many garden centers.

CLUSTER TYPE	FLOWER TYPE	LEAF TYPE	LEAF ATTACHMENT
Round	**Composite**	**Simple**	**Whorl**

131

Joe-pye Weed
Eutrochium maculatum

Family: Aster (Asteraceae)

Height: 2–10' (60–300 cm)

Flower: a large flat cluster, 5–10" (12.5–25 cm) wide, of pinkish purple flowers; hundreds of individual flowers, ¼" (.6 cm) wide, make up each flower head

Leaf: whorls of 3–5 coarsely toothed lance-shaped leaves, each 3–9" (7.5–22.5 cm) long

Bloom: summer

Cycle/Origin: perennial, native

Habitat: wet, sun, meadows, along roads and streams

Range: throughout

Stan's Notes: Sometimes called Spotted Joe-pye Weed because its stem often has purplish spots. Joe-pye Weed is a very tall and robust plant that likes moist soil along streams and wet ditches. Its flowers are very attractive to many species of butterflies, and it makes a good garden plant (it can be purchased at many garden centers). One of several similar species of Joe-pye in Michigan, all of which take their names from Joe Pye, a Native American medicine man. Very similar to Sweet Joe-pye Weed (pg. 131), but with large flower clusters. Like all members of the Aster family, Joe-pye Weed has a head of composite flowers made solely of disk flowers, lacking any ray flowers.

CLUSTER TYPE
Flat

FLOWER TYPE
Composite

LEAF TYPE
Simple

LEAF ATTACHMENT
Whorl

Fireweed
Chamerion angustifolium

Family: Evening Primrose (Onagraceae)

Height: 2–6' (60–180 cm)

Flower: spike cluster, 6–12" (15–30 cm) long, with multiple pinkish purple flowers; individual flowers, 1" (2.5 cm) wide, made up of 4 oval petals; flowers open individually from the bottom of the spike up

Leaf: narrow, faintly toothed, willow-like leaves that grow up to 8" (20 cm) long

Fruit: slender, pod-like containers, up to 3" (7.5 cm) long, open from the top down to release silky down that carries the seeds away on the wind

Bloom: summer, fall

Cycle/Origin: perennial, native

Habitat: dry, shade, along roads, recently burned woodlands, coniferous and deciduous woods

Range: throughout

Stan's Notes: Also called Willow Herb because of its willow-shaped leaves, Fireweed is one of the first plants to grow after a forest fire, hence its common name. It grows individually in disturbed soils or in large masses after the wind has dispersed its seeds into burned areas. A very common wildflower found throughout the world, eight species of Fireweed make their home in Michigan. A good nectar source for many species of butterflies.

CLUSTER TYPE
Spike

FLOWER TYPE
Regular

LEAF TYPE
Simple

LEAF ATTACHMENT
Alternate

FRUIT
Pod

fruit

Bittersweet Nightshade
Solanum dulcamara

Family: Nightshade (Solanaceae)

Height: 2–8' (60–240 cm); vine

Flower: purple flowers, ½" (1 cm) wide, made up of 5 pointed and swept-back petals and resembling a purple (sometimes white) bursting star with a yellow center; its pointed center reminds some of a bird's beak

Leaf: toothless pointed leaves, 3½" (8.5 cm) long; most leaves have 2 small lobes at the base that do not always appear to be part of the main leaf

Fruit: shiny green berries ripen to shades of red

Bloom: spring, summer, fall

Cycle/Origin: perennial, non-native

Habitat: dry, sun and shade, disturbed areas

Range: throughout

Stan's Notes: A weak vine that was introduced into North America from Eurasia, Bittersweet Nightshade is easily identified by its dark purple flowers with yellow centers as well as its rich red berries. It is sometimes called Deadly Nightshade because its leaves and unripe fruit contain the alkaloid solanine. Although the toxin is not fatal, it can cause problems for young children if eaten in any quantity. Closely related to the common garden tomato, this wildflower was dubbed "Bittersweet" because of the taste of its leaves.

FLOWER TYPE
Regular

LEAF TYPE
Simple Lobed

LEAF ATTACHMENT
Alternate

FRUIT
Berry

137

Dame's Rocket
Hesperis matronalis

Family: Mustard (Brassicaceae)

Height: 1–3' (30–90 cm)

Flower: a purple, blue or white flower, ½–1" (1–2.5 cm) wide, with 4 round petals; flower stalks are crowded with flowers and bloom from the bottom up

Leaf: wide, coarsely toothed, lance-shaped leaves, 1–3" (2.5–7.5 cm) long, with short leafstalks; both stems and leaves are covered with fine hairs

Fruit: thin, wiry seed pods, ½–3" (1–7.5 cm) long, that split open lengthwise to release tiny black seeds

Bloom: spring, summer

Cycle/Origin: annual or biennial, non-native

Habitat: wet or dry, sun or shade, along roads, open fields, near old homesteads

Range: throughout

Stan's Notes: Now well established in Michigan, Dame's Rocket, a European native, is a garden escapee that closely resembles Wild Blue Phlox (pg. 55) or garden phlox. Phlox have five petals while Dame's Rocket has only four, as do all members of the Mustard family. Also called Sweet Rocket or Dame's Violet, this usually grows as an annual or biennial; rarely as a perennial. If its flower heads are cut back, it will bloom a second time. Flowers attract nectaring butterflies (especially Tiger Swallowtails), moths and hummingbirds.

FLOWER TYPE **Regular**   LEAF TYPE **Simple**   LEAF ATTACHMENT **Alternate**   FRUIT **Pod**

Swamp Laurel

Kalmia polifolia

Family: Heath (Ericaceae)

Height: 1–3' (30–90 cm); shrub

Flower: lavender, cup-shaped flowers, ¾–1" (2–2.5 cm) wide, cluster near the top of woody stalks; 5 petals fuse to form the cup shape, and each flower has a very long protruding center

Leaf: leathery evergreen leaves, 1–2" (2.5–5 cm) long, grow opposite along a stem with 2 edges; each leaf is just ¼" (.6 cm) wide, and its edges (margins) roll under; no hair underneath leaf

Bloom: spring

Cycle/Origin: perennial, native

Habitat: wet, sun, bogs

Range: northern half of the L.P. and the entire U.P.

Stan's Notes: A woody shrub of wet bogs, Swamp Laurel's stems have two edges and are light tan or gray in color. Its leaves, twigs and flowers are poisonous, so it's important not to confuse it with edible Labrador Tea (pg. 303), which has dense brown hairs underneath. Swamp Laurel has no hairs. The genus name, *Kalmia*, honors the Swedish botanist Pehr Kalm.

FLOWER TYPE
Regular

LEAF TYPE
Simple

LEAF ATTACHMENT
Opposite

141

Great Blue Lobelia

Lobelia siphilitica

Family: Bellflower (Campanulaceae)

Height: 1–4' (30–120 cm)

Flower: many bright purple flowers, 1" (2.5 cm) wide, on a tall leafy stem, 6–12" (15–30 cm) long; each flower has 2 petals (lips), one upper and one lower, lower is striped with white; each flower rising from the axis of the alternate leaves

Leaf: lance shaped leaves, 2–6" (5–15 cm) long, alternate along the stem, usually lacking teeth

Bloom: summer, fall

Cycle/Origin: perennial, native

Habitat: woodland, wet meadows

Range: throughout

Stan's Notes: A tall showy plant of wet woodland, swamps and floodplains, Great Blue Lobelia is similar to the Cardinal Flower (pg. 189), only it has purple instead of red flowers. Attracts hummingbirds for pollination. The species name *siphilitica* comes from the mistaken belief that the alkaloids in the roots can cure syphilis, but actually the alkaloids can cause vomiting. The genus name *Lobelia* honors Flemish botanist Matthias de Lobel (1538–1616).

CLUSTER TYPE **Spike**   FLOWER TYPE **Irregular**   LEAF TYPE **Simple**   LEAF ATTACHMENT **Alternate**

Showy Orchis
Galearis spectabilis

Family: Orchid (Orchidaceae)

Height: 5–12" (12.5–30 cm)

Flower: 12–20 spectacular, two-toned flowers, 1" (2.5 cm) tall, each made up of 2 petals and 3 petal-like sepals that fuse together to form a purplish pink hood that hangs over white lower petals; several flowers grow along a single thick stem

Leaf: 2 long basal leaves, 10" (25 cm) long and up to 3" (7.5 cm) wide, with deeply ribbed parallel veins clasp the stem; flower stem has several smaller lance-shaped leaves, 1–3" (2.5–7.5 cm) long

Bloom: spring

Cycle/Origin: perennial, native

Habitat: wet, sun, swamps, moist woods

Range: southern half of the L.P.

Stan's Notes: A woodland species of orchid with a pleasant fragrance. Unlike the Showy Lady's Slipper (pg. 121), this orchid has a colored hood over a white lower petal. Lower white petal (lip) is a landing platform for pollinating insects that must push hard to get inside. This plant is erratic in its presence in that it may bloom for several years and then disappear or show up some distance away. Many orchids take up to fifteen years to mature and produce flowers. Enjoy these flowers in the wild and don't dig them up.

FLOWER TYPE
Irregular

LEAF TYPE
Simple

LEAF ATTACHMENT
Alternate

LEAF ATTACHMENT
Basal

LEAF ATTACHMENT
Clasping

Spotted Knapweed
Centaurea stoebe

Family: Aster (Asteraceae)

Height: 2–3' (60–90 cm)

Flower: each plant produces 25–100 lavender-to-purple flower heads, 1" (2.5 cm) wide, made entirely of disk flowers; each flower is surrounded underneath by a black-tipped, brown, prickly bract

Leaf: deeply lobed lower leaves, 4–8" (10–20 cm) long, with many narrow lobes; upper leaves (also deeply lobed) are much smaller, 1–2" (2.5–5 cm) long, with very narrow pointed lobes

Bloom: summer, fall

Cycle/Origin: biennial, non-native

Habitat: dry, sun, fields, along roads

Range: throughout

Stan's Notes: Spotted Knapweed is a non-native plant commonly found growing in large groups along the side of the road and in open fields. It looks a lot like the garden annual, Bachelor Button (not shown). Its lavender flowers can range from white to red, but always have the brown triangular bracts. Its leaves often appear wilted and curled, and it is considered a noxious weed by many state agricultural departments because of its aggressiveness in crowding out other plants. Possibly an allelopathic plant that chemically changes the soil so as to discourage other plants and favor its own offspring.

FLOWER TYPE
Composite

LEAF TYPE
Simple Lobed

LEAF ATTACHMENT
Alternate

Wild Bergamot

Monarda fistulosa

Family: Mint (Lamiaceae)

Height: 2–4' (60–120 cm)

Flower: a round cluster, 1–2" (2.5–5 cm) wide, of many individual pale lavender flowers; individual flowers, ¼" (.6 cm) long, are tubular with a lower curved petal and a thin straight petal

Leaf: coarsely toothed, lance-shaped leaves, 1–3" (2.5–7.5 cm) long, grow on short leafstalks

Bloom: summer

Cycle/Origin: perennial, native

Habitat: dry, sun, fields, prairies, along roads

Range: throughout

Stan's Notes: Also called Horsemint or Bee Balm, Wild Bergamot is a tall single-stemmed plant of open fields and prairies. The heads of its lavender flowers attract many insects, including bees, butterflies and beetles. Look for its square stems and opposite pairs of leaves to help identify this member of the Mint family. Emits a strong scent when any part of the plant is rubbed or crushed, and has been used in folk medicine as a mint tea to treat many respiratory and digestive ailments. The common name "Bergamot" refers to a small citrus tree that produces a similar scent and which is an essential flavoring ingredient in Earl Gray tea.

CLUSTER TYPE
Round

FLOWER TYPE
Irregular

LEAF TYPE
Simple

LEAF ATTACHMENT
Opposite

Alfalfa
Medicago sativa

Family: Pea or Bean (Fabaceae)

Height: 1–3' (30–90 cm)

Flower: tight spike clusters, 1–2" (2.5–5 cm) long, of blue-to-purple flowers, each ¼–⅓" (.6–.8 cm) long; flowers have 1 large upper petal and 3 smaller lower petals

Leaf: 3-part clover-like leaf, 1–2" (2.5–5 cm) long

Fruit: green seed pods twist into coils and become nearly black with age

Bloom: spring, summer, fall

Cycle/Origin: perennial, non-native

Habitat: dry, sun, fields, along roads

Range: throughout

Stan's Notes. This deep-rooted perennial is usually found along roads or fields where it has escaped cultivation. Alfalfa is often planted by farmers as a food crop for farm animals and to improve soil fertility (it fixes nitrogen from the air into the soil through its roots). A winter-hardy variety of alfalfa, developed by Wendelin Grimm in Carver County, Minnesota, in the late 1800s, was partially responsible for the establishment of the dairy industry in the upper Midwest in the early 1900s. Alfalfa's thin stems often cause the plant to fall over under its own weight at maturity, leaving it prostrate. Its flower color ranges from light blue to dark purple and it is a prime host plant for the alfalfa butterfly, Orange Sulphur.

CLUSTER TYPE
Spike

FLOWER TYPE
Irregular

LEAF TYPE
Compound

LEAF ATTACHMENT
Alternate

FRUIT
Pod

151

New England Aster
Symphyotrichum novae-angliae

Family: Aster (Asteraceae)

Height: 3–7' (90–210 cm)

Flower: many (25–100) bright purple-and-yellow flowers per plant; individual flower heads, 1–2" (2.5–5 cm) wide, have 35–45 purple petals (ray flowers) with a yellow center (disk flowers); flower stalks are covered with sticky hairs

Leaf: many long, toothless, stalkless lance-shaped leaves, 1–5" (2.5–12.5 cm) long, that clasp the stem; leaves are large near the base and extremely small near the flowers

Bloom: fall

Cycle/Origin: perennial, native

Habitat: moist, sun, prairies, along roads

Range: throughout

Stan's Notes: A large, showy, autumn-flowering plant, New England Aster features highly variable flower color, ranging from pink to lavender or from blue to white, although it usually presents a rich purple. Its stems are often hairy and crowded with clasping leaves; leaves near the ground fall off early, leaving "naked legs." It is often grown in gardens. A great nectar plant for its long bloom time in autumn. Heavily visited by migrating Monarch butterflies.

FLOWER TYPE
Composite

LEAF TYPE
Simple

LEAF ATTACHMENT
Alternate

LEAF ATTACHMENT
Clasping

153

Wild Geranium
Geranium maculatum

Family: Geranium (Geraniaceae)

Height: 1–2' (30–60 cm)

Flower: group of 2–10 regular lavender flowers; individual flowers, 1–2" (2.5–5 cm) wide, are made up of 5 heavily veined lavender petals

Leaf: basal leaves, 4–5" (10–12.5 cm) long, on long stalks; leaves are coarsely toothed and deeply veined with 5–7 elongated lobes; only 2–3 stem leaves (cauline) per plant

Fruit: elongated, beak-like, pod-like container that splits lengthwise to release many seeds

Bloom: spring

Cycle/Origin: perennial, native

Habitat: dry, shade, deciduous woods, meadows

Range: southern half of the L.P.

Stan's Notes: A common spring-blooming perennial of shady deciduous woodlands. The Wild Geranium's delicate lavender flowers rise above its many-lobed leaves. Its seed capsules split into five long and curled sections to release seeds. Its genus name, *Geranium*, comes from the Greek *geranos* (a crane), and describes its seed capsule's long narrow shape like that of the bill of a crane. It is also called Crane's-bill Geranium.

FLOWER TYPE
Regular

LEAF TYPE
Simple Lobed

LEAF ATTACHMENT
Basal

LEAF ATTACHMENT
Opposite

FRUIT
Pod

Beach Pea
Lathyrus japonicus

Family: Pea or Bean (Fabaceae)

Height: 1–2' (30–60 cm)

Flower: spike cluster, 1–3" (2.5–7.5 cm) long, of 3–10 pea-like purple-red flowers, ¾" (2 cm) wide; flowers can range in color from pink to purple

Leaf: compound leaf, 3–6" (7.5–15 cm) long, with up to 6 pairs (12 total) pointed fleshy leaflets, 1–2" (2.5–5 cm) long, per leaf; has a large distinctive pair of leaves at base of each leaf (stipules) and a forked tendril used to climb onto other plants

Fruit: elongated pea-like pod

Bloom: summer

Cycle/Origin: perennial, native

Habitat: sandy beaches

Range: surrounding the Great Lakes

Stan's Notes: A common plant along sandy beaches, usually around the Great Lakes. Rarely found inland. The stems are arching, with ends of the upper leaves modified into fork tendrils that wrap around stems of other plants. Look for the very large leaf-like stipules at the base of the leafstalk. Not only is this plant found around the Great Lakes, it is also found along the Pacific Coast.

CLUSTER TYPE
Spike

FLOWER TYPE
Irregular

LEAF TYPE
Compound

LEAF ATTACHMENT
Opposite

FRUIT
Pod

Field Thistle
Cirsium discolor

Family: Aster (Asteraceae)

Height: 3–5' (90–150 cm)

Flower: pale purple flower heads, 2" (5 cm) wide, with a large, green, spiny base; each flower head (5–20 per plant) is closely clasped by a set of leaves (bracts)

Leaf: elongated, spine-tipped, lobed leaves, 6–12" (15–30 cm) long, clasp the stem; the underside of each leaf is densely covered with white hairs

Bloom: summer

Cycle/Origin: perennial, native

Habitat: dry, sun, open fields, along roads

Range: throughout the L.P.

Stan's Notes: The white "wool" under its clasping leaves and the set of small leaves just beneath each flower help to positively identify the Field Thistle, one of many thistles found in Michigan. Each plant produces many pale purple flower heads on only a few stalks. The plant is a favorite of bees and wasps, who sip nectar and in turn pollinate the flower. A good nectar plant for attracting Tiger Swallowtails and Monarch butterflies. Often confused with Bull Thistle (pg. 183), but the Field Thistle leaves are not nearly as prickly and its flower is much paler.

FLOWER TYPE
Composite

LEAF TYPE
Simple Lobed

LEAF ATTACHMENT
Alternate

LEAF ATTACHMENT
Clasping

Hoary Vervain
Verbena stricta

Family: Vervain (Verbenaceae)

Height: 1–3' (30–90 cm)

Flower: usually a single spike, 2–5" (5–12.5 cm) long, of purple-to-blue tube-like flowers, ½" (1 cm) long, but it can have multiple flower stalks; each flower is made up of 5 fused petals

Leaf: oval leaves, 2–3" (5–7.5 cm) long, are thick and covered with dense whitish hairs; they lack a leafstalk but do not actually clasp its square stem

Bloom: summer

Cycle/Origin: perennial, native

Habitat: dry, fields, along ditches, shores, roadsides

Range: throughout the L.P.

Stan's Notes: Hoary Vervain is a tall slender plant, sometimes with multiple, pencil-thin flower spikes that bloom from the bottom up. Its stems are square with opposite leaves, which is why it is often confused with a member of the Mint family. The genus name, *Verbena*, is Latin for "sacred plant," and refers to an ancient time when the plant was thought to have medicinal properties. Its flowers can be rosy but are usually more purple than the blue flowers of the Blue Vervain (pg. 57).

CLUSTER TYPE   LEAF TYPE   LEAF ATTACHMENT
Spike   **Simple**   **Opposite**

Purple Coneflower
Echinacea purpurea

Family: Aster (Asteraceae)

Height: 2–3' (60–90 cm)

Flower: large flower heads, 3–5" (7.5–12.5 cm) wide, made up of 14–20 droopy pinkish purple (sometimes white) petals (ray flowers) that surround a cone-shaped, spiny, orange center (disk flowers)

Leaf: coarsely toothed, 3-veined leaves, 5" (12.5 cm) wide and up to 8" (20 cm) long; leaves are rough to the touch because of many small hairs

Bloom: summer, fall

Cycle/Origin: perennial, native

Habitat: dry, sun, prairies, along roads, ditches

Range: mainly associated with cities, where it has escaped from gardens

Stan's Notes: A tall showy flower of the prairies, Purple Coneflower is a popular plant for herbal remedies. Its leaves and stems are rough to touch because of stiff hairs covering the plant. The American Goldfinch finds its seed heads irresistible, and the plant is also a favorite of many butterfly species that visit to sip nectar. The genus name comes from the Greek *echinos*, meaning "spiny," and refers to its dry, spiny seed heads. There are at least ten species of coneflowers. A summer bloomer, it is commonly grown in gardens. Many flowers found in the wild are garden escapees.

FLOWER TYPE
Composite

LEAF TYPE
Simple

LEAF ATTACHMENT
Alternate

163

Purple Fringed Orchid
Platanthera psycodes

Family: Orchid (Orchidaceae)

Height: 1–2' (30–60 cm)

Flower: a thick spike, 6–10" (15–25 cm) long, of many lavender-to-purple flowers, ½–1" (1–2.5 cm) wide, each made up of 1 upper petal and 3 lower petals with many fine notches that form a fringe

Leaf: linear tulip-like leaves, up to 8" (20 cm) long, stand erect from the base; thinner, parallel-veined stem leaves, up to 4" (10 cm) long, clasp the stem

Bloom: summer

Cycle/Origin: perennial, native

Habitat: wet, sun, grassy marshes, damp woodland borders

Range: throughout

Stan's Notes: "Fringed" in the common name refers to the petal edges. Each flower petal has a long spur at its base. Pollination occurs when moths insert their tongues into flowers and emerge with sticky pollen sacks, called pollinia, that they unwittingly carry to other flowers. The plant gets its nourishment through a specific fungal relationship (mycorrhiza), which (so far) has not been cultivated; thus it won't grow in a garden and should never be transplanted. Please do not pick this flower—enjoy it with your eyes and camera only.

CLUSTER TYPE
Spike

FLOWER TYPE
Irregular

LEAF TYPE
Simple

LEAF ATTACHMENT
Alternate

LEAF ATTACHMENT
Basal

Rough Blazing Star
Liatris aspera

Family: Aster (Asteraceae)

Height: 16–48" (40–120 cm)

Flower: a single tall stem, 6–12" (15–30 cm) long, of many round, purple flower heads, each ¾" (2 cm) wide, and made up of 25–40 florets (disk flowers); both stalkless and stalked flower heads occur on 1 stem, and each flower head is surrounded by flat rounded bracts

Leaf: thin lance-shaped leaves, ¼" (.6 cm) wide and 4–12" (10–30 cm) long, alternate along the stem; upper leaves become progressively smaller near the top

Bloom: summer, fall

Cycle/Origin: perennial, native

Habitat: dry, sun, sandy soils, prairies

Range: southern half of the L.P.

Stan's Notes: One of seven blazing star species in Michigan, Rough Blazing Star is distinguished by its round, flat flower bracts and rough feel (*aspera* is Latin for "rough"). Relished by deer and cattle, its flowers have distinct spaces between each flower head. A major nectar source for fall-migrating Monarch butterflies. Unlike other floral spikes, its flowers bloom from top to bottom. Blazing stars are strictly North American, and all species are in cultivation.

CLUSTER TYPE   FLOWER TYPE   LEAF TYPE   LEAF ATTACHMENT
Spike   **Composite**   **Simple**   **Alternate**

Purple Loosestrife

Lythrum salicaria

Family: Loosestrife (Lythraceae)

Height: 2–5' (60–150 cm)

Flower: a long spike cluster, 1–2' (30–60 cm), of pinkish purple flowers; each flower, ½–¾" (1–2 cm) wide, is made up of 4–6 petals, rising on short stalks near the leaf attachment

Leaf: mostly opposite, but often whorled in 3s and 4s, narrow lance-shaped leaves, 1–4" (2.5–10 cm) long; leaves nearly clasp the stem and are smaller near the top

Bloom: summer

Cycle/Origin: perennial, non-native

Habitat: wet, sun, quiet waters, ponds, marshes, swamps

Range: throughout the L.P. and scattered widely in the U.P.

Stan's Notes: A very showy plant that often grows in large numbers, Purple Loosestrife puts on an impressive show in bloom. One of the few plants that has both opposite and whorled leaves on the same plant, it was once grown as a garden plant because of its striking purple flower spikes. This native of Eurasia is often considered a noxious weed because it takes over and pushes out native plants, such as cattails and bulrushes. Each flower spike can produce up to 300,000 seeds; it also reproduces new shoots from its roots. Efforts are underway to reduce the loosestrife population by releasing special beetles that feed on the plant's roots and leaves.

CLUSTER TYPE
Spike

FLOWER TYPE
Regular

LEAF TYPE
Simple

LEAF ATTACHMENT
Opposite

LEAF ATTACHMENT
Whorl

169

Spotted Coralroot
Corallorhiza maculata

Family: Orchid (Orchidaceae)

Height: 6–20" (15–50 cm)

Flower: a single, leafless, red stem produces 20–40 red, yellow and white flowers, ¾" (2 cm) tall; each flower is made up of 5 petal-like sepals that surround a white lower petal (lip) with purple spots

Leaf: no leaves; tubular sheaths up to 3" (7.5 cm) long

Fruit: nodding pod-like container, 1" (2.5 cm) long

Bloom: summer

Cycle/Origin: perennial, native

Habitat: wet, shade, coniferous woods

Range: throughout

Stan's Notes: An unusual orchid, Spotted Coralroot is often described as a leafless red stalk with many flowers. It usually grows in groups of up to ten stems. It lacks chlorophyll, and is instead nourished through a partnership with an underground fungus (mycorrhiza) that breaks down dead organic matter (saprophytic) for the plant to feed on. Since it doesn't make food from sunlight, this orchid lacks traditional leaves, and instead has only sheaths. One of four species of coral orchid in Michigan, its common name comes from its coral-shaped roots. Please don't pick or try to transplant. It won't grow in gardens.

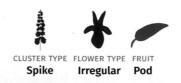

CLUSTER TYPE   FLOWER TYPE   FRUIT
Spike   **Irregular**   **Pod**

Red Clover
Trifolium pratense

Family: Pea or Bean (Fabaceae)

Height: 6–24" (15–60 cm)

Flower: round clusters of 50–100 purple-to-rosy red flowers, ⅛–¼" (.3–.6 cm) long, that appear as 1 large red flower, 1" (2.5 cm) wide

Leaf: typical clover leaf, ½–2" (1–5 cm) wide; made up of 3 leaflets; each leaflet has white markings in a V-shape (chevron)

Bloom: spring, summer, fall

Cycle/Origin: perennial, non-native

Habitat: wet or dry, sun, old fields, pastures

Range: throughout

Stan's Notes: A native of Europe, Red Clover was introduced to North America as a hay and pasture crop. It has since escaped to the wild and is now one of the most common roadside plants. It is still grown as a rotation crop to improve the soil fertility because its roots fix nitrogen into the soil. The genus name, *Trifolium*, means "three leaves," which describes the three leaflets, while the species name, *pratense*, means "meadows" and refers to where you find it growing. In agricultural settings, it's usually pollinated by honeybees, but in the wild, it's pollinated by bumblebees. Without these insects, it is unable to produce seeds and will eventually die out. Seeds can lay dormant for years before sprouting.

CLUSTER TYPE
Round

FLOWER TYPE
Irregular

LEAF TYPE
Compound

LEAF ATTACHMENT
Alternate

173

Indian Paintbrush
Castilleja coccinea

Family: Broomrape (Orobanchaceae)

Height: 1–2' (30–60 cm)

Flower: inconspicuous greenish yellow flowers, 1" (2.5 cm) long, interspersed among a cluster of bright, 3-lobed, red-tipped, leafy bracts that are often mistaken for the flower petals

Leaf: single hairy stem; nearly clasping alternate leaves usually divided into 3 narrow, finger-like lobes

Fruit: small, pod-like container, ¾" (2 cm) long, contains many brown seeds

Bloom: spring, summer

Cycle/Origin: annual, native

Habitat: moist, open fields, prairies, rocky outcroppings

Range: throughout

Stan's Notes: Named "Paintbrush" because each stem is topped with scarlet, resembling a painter's brush. A member of the Broomrape family, also called Painted Cup due to its cup-shaped vermilion bracts. Thought to be semiparasitic, its roots tap into other plant roots for nutrients. This most colorful of Michigan wildflowers is also found in a less common yellow variety. Is among about 110 species of paintbrush in North America. Only a few species occur in the eastern U.S. Legend has it that it sprang up where a Native American discarded his brushes after painting a scarlet sunset.

FLOWER TYPE
Tube

LEAF TYPE
Simple Lobed

LEAF ATTACHMENT
Alternate

FRUIT
Pod

175

Striped Coralroot
Corallorhiza maculata

Family: Orchid (Orchidaceae)

Height: 8–20" (20–50 cm)

Flower: a single, leafless stem with many reddish purple flowers, 1–1¼" (2.5–3 cm) wide, crowded along the stem; upper petals are striped or sometimes all reddish purple; lower center petal wider, thicker and lacking stripes

Leaf: reduced to tiny sheaths or scales near the base of the single stem

Fruit: backward-curving pod

Bloom: spring, summer

Cycle/Origin: perennial, native

Habitat: coniferous woods, cedar swamps

Range: northern half of the L.P. and the entire U.P.

Stan's Notes: A single-stem orchid that some say is the most attractive of the four species in Michigan. A northern species that cannot tolerate transplanting and will not grow in the southern part of the state. Lacks any chlorophyll, obtaining its nutrients from the dead organic material in the soil. Named Coralroot from the numerous branched underground roots that appear like coral. May occur singly or in large clumps of over a dozen or more.

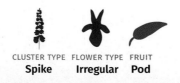

CLUSTER TYPE
Spike

FLOWER TYPE
Irregular

FRUIT
Pod

fruit

Columbine
Aquilegia canadensis

Family: Buttercup (Ranunculaceae)

Height: 1–2' (30–60 cm)

Flower: a collection of 5 upside-down red-orange tubes forms a bell, 1–2" (2.5–5 cm) long, with yellow tips and hollow nectar-filled spurs

Leaf: long-stalked leaves, 4–6" (10–15 cm) long, divided into 9–27 thin, light green leaflets; each leaflet has 3 lobes

Fruit: papery pod-like container that splits along its side to release many shiny round seeds

Bloom: spring, summer

Cycle/Origin: perennial, native

Habitat: dry, shady, rocky places, open deciduous woods

Range: throughout

Stan's Notes: Children often mistake the Columbine for Honeysuckle and bite off its long spurs to suck out the nectar. While there is only one native species in Michigan, numerous cultivated species have escaped into the wild. This plant was once considered for our national wildflower because its flower resembles the Bald Eagle's talons; *Aquilegia* is Latin for "eagle." Its nectar tubes make it a favorite flower of hummingbirds and long-tongued moths; some insects chew holes in its tubes, cheating to get a little nectar. Grows well in a garden. Collect only seeds; don't dig up the plant.

FLOWER TYPE
Bell

LEAF TYPE
Compound

LEAF ATTACHMENT
Alternate

FRUIT
Pod

Red Trillium
Trillium erectum

Family: Bunchflower (Melanthiaceae)

Height: 8–24" (20–60 cm)

Flower: single dull red flower, 1–2" (2.5–5 cm) wide, stands on an erect stalk several inches above the leaves; each flower has 3 pointed red-to-maroon petals and 3 sharply pointed green sepals

Leaf: 3 single dark green leaves, 3–4" (7.5–10 cm) long, in a whorl around a single stem; each leaf has a network of veins

Fruit: single reddish berry

Bloom: spring

Cycle/Origin: perennial, native

Habitat: dry woodland

Range: scattered throughout the L.P.

Stan's Notes: One of the more common trilliums. Also known as Wakerobin, Purple Trillium or Stinking Benjamin. Flowers smell of carrion and attract flies, which pollinate inadvertently. Species name *erectum* refers to its erect flower stalk, while common name "Wakerobin" refers to a totally different group of plants in Europe, the Arum family. Apparently trilliums are mistakenly identified as belonging to that group of plants. The ill-smelling flowers were used to treat ill-smelling ailments, such as gangrene.

FLOWER TYPE
Regular

LEAF TYPE
Simple

LEAF ATTACHMENT
Whorl

FRUIT
Berry

flower

Bull Thistle
Cirsium vulgare

Family: Aster (Asteraceae)

Height: 2–6' (60–180 cm)

Flower: large, red-to-purple flower heads, 1½–2" (4–5 cm) wide, sit on a wide green base that narrows near its center; 1 to several flower heads per stem

Leaf: narrow leaves, 3–6" (7.5–15 cm) long, with many lobes, each ending in a sharp spine

Bloom: summer, fall

Cycle/Origin: biennial, non-native

Habitat: dry, open fields, sun, disturbed soils

Range: throughout

Stan's Notes: The spiniest of the many different thistle species found in Michigan, the Bull Thistle is a true biennial, producing a low rosette of leaves its first year and sending up a tall flower stalk in the second. A favorite flower of large bees, the Bull Thistle's little seeds feature tiny, parachute-like thistledown to carry them off on the winds after pollination. The seeds are a favorite food of American Goldfinches, which use the thistledown to line their nests and, therefore, must wait until late summer to raise their young. Often confused with Field Thistle (pg. 159), Bull Thistle has a much deeper reddish purple flower and more spines on its leaves.

FLOWER TYPE
Composite

LEAF TYPE
Simple Lobed

LEAF ATTACHMENT
Alternate

leaf

Pitcher Plant
Sarracenia purpurea

Family: Pitcher Plant (Sarraceniaceae)

Height: 8–24" (20–60 cm)

Flower: a large, maroon-to-deep red, bell-shaped flower, 2–3" (5–7.5 cm) wide, droops from a single, tall, leafless stalk; 5 petals and 5 petal-like sepals form the bell shape

Leaf: a single stalkless leaf forms a long hollow tube to hold rainwater with a large lip on its upper edge

Fruit: round pod-like capsule containing seeds

Bloom: summer

Cycle/Origin: perennial, native

Habitat: wet, bogs

Range: throughout

Stan's Notes: A water plant of acid bogs, the Pitcher Plant gets some of its nutrients from the soil and some from insects that it captures. Its leaves form a tall tube or funnel that fills with rainwater, and downward-pointing hairs line the opening of the tube. This allows insects to travel down but not up; unsuspecting bugs are thereby captured. The plant secretes enzymes into the rainwater, which helps it to digest any insect that falls into the watery trap. The plant then absorbs the nutrients, especially nitrogen, which is otherwise nearly inaccessible in bog soils because of the high acidity.

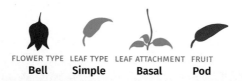

FLOWER TYPE **Bell** LEAF TYPE **Simple** LEAF ATTACHMENT **Basal** FRUIT **Pod**

fruit

Swamp Milkweed
Asclepias incarnata

Family: Dogbane (Apocynaceae)

Height: 1–4' (30–120 cm)

Flower: pinkish red-and-white flowers, ¼" (.6 cm) wide, form several flat clusters, 2–3" (5–7.5 cm) wide; individual flowers have 5 downward-curving petals and 5 upward petals, resembling a crown

Leaf: narrow opposite leaves, ½" (1 cm) wide, and up to 4" (10 cm) long; short leafstalk and no teeth

Fruit: elongated narrow pod, 2–4" (5–10 cm) long, opens along one side to release 10–20 brown, disk-shaped seeds, each with white tuft

Bloom: summer

Cycle/Origin: perennial, native

Habitat: wet, sun, swamps, streams, wet meadows

Range: throughout

Stan's Notes: This plant usually has one long stem that branches near the top into several flat-topped flower clusters. Its upper stems often turn rosy red, matching its flowers. Each flower has a slit allowing an insect's legs to slip inside and emerge with a pair of pollen sacs that will pollinate another flower. So, only a few flowers become pollinated. This milkweed has less milky sap than others, but it has been used in folk medicine for a variety of ailments. A host and nectar plant for Monarchs and a good plant for a butterfly garden.

CLUSTER TYPE	FLOWER TYPE	LEAF TYPE	LEAF ATTACHMENT	FRUIT
Flat	**Irregular**	**Simple**	**Opposite**	**Pod**

Cardinal Flower
Lobelia cardinalis

Family: Bellflower (Campanulaceae)

Height: 2–4' (60–120 cm)

Flower: a tall open spike, 1–2' (30–60 cm) long, of scarlet-red flowers, 1½" (4 cm) wide, that alternate on a stem, with the bottom flowers opening before the upper; 5 narrow petals, 2 upper and 3 spreading lower, unite to form a thin tube at its base

Leaf: toothed, lance-shaped leaves, up to 6" (15 cm) long, nearly clasp the stem

Bloom: summer, fall

Cycle/Origin: perennial, native

Habitat: wet, shade, along streams and wetlands, swamps

Range: throughout the L.P.

Stan's Notes: By far one of the most spectacular wildflowers of Michigan, the Cardinal Flower is found growing in small patches along Michigan's streams and rivers. These flowers can be grown in gardens, but its roots need to be wet and its flowers must have some sunlight. The Cardinal Flower is not very successful at reproducing, perhaps because it can only be pollinated by hummingbirds. Do not dig this plant from the wild (it can be purchased at garden centers). While it occasionally produces white or rose-colored blooms, its scarlet-red flowers resemble the bright red color of the robes worn by Roman Catholic cardinals, thus providing its common name.

CLUSTER TYPE	FLOWER TYPE	LEAF TYPE	LEAF ATTACHMENT
Spike	**Irregular**	**Simple**	**Alternate**

Bastard Toadflax
Comandra umbellata

Family: Sandalwood (Santalaceae)

Height: 6–16" (15–40 cm)

Flower: several compact, flat clusters, 1–2" (2.5–5 cm) wide, of white flowers; individual flowers, ⅛" (.5 cm) long; 5 petal-like sepals fuse at base

Leaf: small oval leaves, ¾–1½" (2–4 cm) wide, alternately line the stem; pale green underneath

Bloom: spring, summer

Growth: perennial, native

Habitat: dry, open fields

Range: throughout

Stan's Notes: Bastard Toadflax is a semiparasitic plant, obtaining some of its nutrients from the roots of other plants, although it also uses the sun to perform photosynthesis to make its own food. Its greenish white flowers lack any regular petals, instead displaying modified leaves (sepals). The name "Toad" has in the past been used to describe any plant that grows in the shade, but it also might come from "tod" (a clump or tuft), which certainly describes this plant's flowering habit. This wildflower forms colonies along horizontal underground roots (rhizomes).

CLUSTER TYPE
Flat

FLOWER TYPE
Regular

LEAF TYPE
Simple

LEAF ATTACHMENT
Alternate

Common Chickweed
Stellaria media

Family: Pink (Caryophyllaceae)

Height: 3–9" (7.5–22.5 cm)

Flower: star-shaped, 5-petaled, white flowers, ¼" (.6 cm) wide, found singly at the end of a tiny stalk; each petal is deeply divided, giving the appearance of 2 petals and making the flower look as though it actually has 10 petals

Leaf: small, simple, toothless pointed leaves, ½–1" (1–2.5 cm) long, sit opposite one other on the stem; the upper leaves clasp the stem, while the lower leaves attach by short thin stalks that are often covered with tiny hairs

Bloom: spring, summer, fall

Cycle/Origin: annual, non-native

Habitat: wet or dry, sun or shade, a plant of gardens and especially lawns or disturbed soil

Range: throughout

Stan's Notes: A common weak-stemmed plant that lays across the ground in large mats, the Common Chickweed displays many flowers per plant and when open, its white flowers look like a sky full of tiny stars. Gardeners are often pestered by the prodigious growth of this annual, which is easily pulled out of the ground. One of six species of chickweed in Michigan, the Common Chickweed is the only non-native and the most widespread.

FLOWER TYPE
Regular

LEAF TYPE
Simple

LEAF ATTACHMENT
Opposite

Narrow-leaved Bluets
Houstonia longifolia

Family: Madder (Rubiaceae)

Height: 5–10" (12.5–25 cm)

Flower: several tiny white-to-pink or lavender tube-shaped flowers, ¼" (.6 cm) wide, arranged at the top of a single thin stem; each flower has 4 pointed petals

Leaf: narrow opposite leaves, ½" (1 cm) long and ¼" (.6 cm) wide, on long thin stems; leaves are often clustered where the stem branches

Bloom: spring, summer

Cycle/Origin: perennial, native

Habitat: prairies

Range: throughout the I P

Stan's Notes: A strikingly beautiful flower of prairies and open places. It often forms small tufted patches of white flowers from pink flower buds. The flower fuses into a tube just below the four pointed petals. Twenty-eight different types of bluets grow in North America and all are recognized by their low growth habit, tubular flowers that flare out into four pointed petals, and opposite leaves on the stem.

FLOWER TYPE **Tube**   LEAF TYPE **Simple**   LEAF ATTACHMENT **Opposite**

Bog Rosemary

Andromeda polifolia var. *latifolia*

Family: Heath (Ericaceae)

Height: 1–2' (30–60 cm); shrub

Flower: a small cluster of 1–4 bell-shaped, white-to-pink flowers, ¼–½" (.8–1 cm) long, sits at the end of an arching woody stem; 5 petals fuse together to form an urn-shaped flower with a very narrow opening

Leaf: narrow, toothless, evergreen leaves 1–2" (2.5–5 cm) long, alternate along the woody stem; each leaf has conspicuous white hairs underneath when young; turns a light brown with age

Fruit: round, pink, pod-like container that dries to brown

Bloom: spring, summer

Cycle/Origin: perennial, native

Habitat: wet, acid bogs and muskegs, usually within coniferous woods

Range: throughout

Stan's Notes: A common woody shrub of Michigan, the Bog Rosemary can often be seen along edges of streams and occasionally in drier places. Its evergreen leaves have an inward-rolled leaf edge (margin). Similar to Labrador Tea (pg. 303).

FLOWER TYPE **Bell** LEAF TYPE **Simple** LEAF ATTACHMENT **Alternate** FRUIT **Pod**

fruit

Wintergreen
Gaultheria procumbens

Family: Heath (Ericaceae); shrub

Height: 2–6" (5–15 cm)

Flower: nodding, white (sometimes pink) bell-shaped flowers, ⅓" (.8 cm) long, consisting of 5 fused petals; 1–3 flowers per plant

Leaf: smooth (but leathery), round fine-toothed, evergreen leaves, 1–2" (2.5–5 cm) wide, often dark, shiny, waxy

Fruit: bright red pulpy berry with a strong wintergreen taste

Bloom: spring, summer

Cycle/Origin: perennial, native

Habitat: dry, shade, coniferous woods

Range: throughout

Stan's Notes: Also called Teaberry or Checkerberry, Wintergreen is a low, creeping, evergreen shrub with leathery leaves. Every part of the plant is strongly aromatic and has been used to flavor teas, candies and medicines. The plant contains methyl salicylate, an oil closely related to aspirin that has a similar effect. Its red berries are edible. The current year's leaves are bright green while those of previous years are brownish green. Leaves stay on the plant and remain green under the snow. Fruit is eaten by birds and wildlife. Often associated with white pines, preferring an acidic, well-drained soil.

FLOWER TYPE **Bell**   LEAF TYPE **Simple**   LEAF ATTACHMENT **Alternate**   FRUIT **Berry**

Goldthread

Coptis trifolia

Family: Buttercup (Ranunculaceae)

Height: 3–6" (7.5–15 cm)

Flower: many single white flowers, ½" (1 cm) wide, with 5–7 narrow petal-like sepals; inconspicuous small petals have numerous feathery flower parts in the center; each flower is on a single thin stalk, usually well above the leaves

Leaf: shiny leaves, 1–2" (2.5–5 cm) wide, palmately divided into 3 leaflets, with each leaflet ½–¾" (1–2 cm) wide; 3-lobed leaflets with scalloped teeth, each on a single basal stalk rising from a thin underground stem (rhizome) that is golden in color

Fruit: 4–6 brown pods arranged in a circle; each pod splits open along one side, releasing seeds

Bloom: spring

Cycle/Origin: perennial, native

Habitat: bogs, wet woodland

Range: throughout

Stan's Notes: A low creeping plant of wet woodland and bogs. It spreads along the forest floor by thread-like, golden-colored roots, hence the common name. Each leaf is shiny, smooth and remains evergreen over winter. The underground stems were chewed to treat mouth sores, hence its other common name, Canker-root.

FLOWER TYPE
Regular

LEAF TYPE
Simple Lobed

LEAF TYPE
Palmate

LEAF ATTACHMENT
Basal

Cut-leaved Toothwort
Cardamine concatenata

Family: Mustard (Brassicaceae)

Height: 8–10" (20–25 cm)

Flower: a small collection of 3–15 regular white or pale lavender flowers, ½" (1 cm) long, each with 4 petals

Leaf: a whorl of 3-lobed leaves; each leaf, 2–5" (5–12.5 cm) wide, has 3 main lobes and many coarse teeth

Fruit: a narrow, upturned pod-like capsule

Bloom: spring

Cycle/Origin: perennial, native

Habitat: shade, deciduous woods

Range: throughout, except for the northeastern L.P.

Stan's Notes: One of the spring ephemeral wildflowers (it flowers early, before the leaves of the forest trees sprout and block out sunlight). Cut-leaved Toothwort grows in small patches that dot the floor of deciduous woods. It dies back to the ground by mid-summer. "Cut-leaved" and "Tooth" refer to the deeply cut lobes of the leaves, which resemble teeth, and "wort" means "plant." A host plant for the Checkered White butterfly caterpillar.

FLOWER TYPE
Regular

LEAF TYPE
Simple Lobed

LEAF ATTACHMENT
Whorl

FRUIT
Pod

Star Flower
Trientalis borealis

Family: Primrose (Primulaceae)

Height: 4–8" (10–20 cm)

Flower: usually only 1–2 star-shaped, white flowers, ½" (1 cm) wide, rise on thin delicate stalks above leaves; individual flowers have 7 sharply pointed petals

Leaf: a single whorl of 5–7 lance-shaped leaves, 2–4" (5–10 cm) long, at the top of a delicate stalk

Fruit: a 5-sided pod-like capsule that contains many seeds

Bloom: spring, summer

Cycle/Origin: perennial, native

Habitat: wet, shade, coniferous woods, deciduous woods

Range: throughout

Stan's Notes: The Star Flower is a small, delicate plant that grows in moist areas, often with mosses and usually in clumps or clusters. Its seven petals are unusual in the plant world. Its common name comes from its pointed petals, which form a star. Its genus name, *Trientalis*, comes from the Latin word meaning "one-third of a foot," referring to the height of the plant. The species name, *borealis*, comes from the Latin word meaning "northern," referring to its northern growing range, which is throughout Canada, reaching down into the U.S.

FLOWER TYPE
Regular

LEAF TYPE
Simple

LEAF ATTACHMENT
Whorl

FRUIT
Pod

False Rue Anemone

Enemion biternatum

Family: Buttercup (Ranunculaceae)

Height: 4–16" (10–40 cm)

Flower: simple 5-petal flowers, ½" (1 cm) wide, white on thin stalks; flowers are single or in clusters at the ends of stalks that rise from the leaf axis

Leaf: set of 3 leaflets; each leaflet is 3-lobed, ½" (1 cm) long

Bloom: spring

Cycle/Origin: perennial, native

Habitat: wet, moist woods

Range: southern half of the L.P.

Stan's Notes: Both False Rue Anemone and true anemones belong to the Buttercup family. Grows from a thick fibrous root that contains a lot of small tubers. Leaves are similar in shape to Rue Anemone (pg. 235), but the False Rue Anemone is taller and has leaves with three deep divisions (lobes). Grows in moist woodland or flood forests, where it sometimes carpets the entire forest floor in spring. Not a true anemone, it's a member of the Buttercup family.

FLOWER TYPE
Regular

LEAF TYPE
Compound

LEAF ATTACHMENT
Whorl

Daisy Fleabane
Erigeron annuus

Family: Aster (Asteraceae)

Height: 1–5' (30–150 cm)

Flower: small white (sometimes pink) flower heads, ½" (1 cm) wide; up to 40 tiny petals (ray flowers) with a yellow center (disk flowers); individual plants can hold up to 30 flower heads

Leaf: thin, finely toothed, lance-shaped, hairy leaves, up to 5" (12.5 cm) long, alternate along a noticeably hairy stem; most leaves lack a stalk and larger leaves are clasping

Bloom: spring, summer, fall

Cycle/Origin: annual, native

Habitat: wet or dry, sun or shade, coniferous woods, deciduous woods, old fields

Range: throughout

Stan's Notes: One of the first asters to bloom each spring, continuing to flower until autumn. An erect plant with thin hairy stems, often growing along roads and edges of woods. Its common name comes from its daisy-like flowers which, when dried, were once believed to keep away fleas. The genus name *Erigeron* comes from the Greek *eri* for "early" and *geron* for "old man," referring to the plant's early blooming and silvery appearance of its hairy stems. At least seven species of fleabane are found in Michigan. Differentiated from other white-flowered asters by lack of leaves on flower stalks.

FLOWER TYPE **Composite** LEAF TYPE **Simple** LEAF ATTACHMENT **Alternate**

Rattlesnake Root
Prenanthes alba

Family: Aster (Asteraceae)

Height: 2–5' (60–150 cm)

Flower: small, white-to-cream-colored and purple-tinged bell-shaped flowers, ½" (1 cm) long, hang in clusters of 3–4; individual flowers have 8–15 petals

Leaf: large, coarsely toothed, triangular-shaped leaves, up to 8" (20 cm) long; leaves have multiple sharp lobes and are highly variable, with some leaves lacking lobes

Bloom: summer, fall

Cycle/Origin: perennial, native

Habitat: wet, shade, deciduous woods

Range: throughout

Stan's Notes: Rattlesnake Root's characteristic leaves and purplish green stems help identify this plant of moist woodlands. One of three species of *Prenanthes* found in Michigan, it is also called White Lettuce. The common name, Rattlesnake Root, comes from its history of use as a snakebite remedy. The sap from its roots and stem was sometimes used to treat dysentery.

FLOWER TYPE
Bell

LEAF TYPE
Simple Lobed

LEAF ATTACHMENT
Alternate

single

Indian Pipe
Monotropa uniflora

Family: Heather (Ericaceae)

Height: 3–9" (7.5–22.5 cm)

Flower: a single, waxy, white (sometimes pink) bell-like flower, ½–1" (1–2.5 cm) long, hangs from the end of each white stem; the hanging bells are formed by 4–5 petals

Leaf: very small scale-like leaves, ¼" (.6 cm) long, often go unnoticed

Fruit: oval pod-like capsule that turns black as seeds mature

Bloom: summer

Cycle/Origin: perennial, native

Habitat: dry, shade, coniferous woods, deciduous woods

Range: throughout

Stan's Notes: A unique plant of the forest, the Indian Pipe lacks chlorophyll, so it always appears white and turns black with age or if picked. It doesn't make food for itself like other plants, and instead gets its nourishment from dead or decaying plant material through a mutually beneficial fungal relationship called mycorrhiza. Some believe it might be a parasitic plant, living off other living plants, killing its host. It often grows in small clumps but can grow alone. The species name, *uniflora*, means "one flower," describing its one bell flower per plant. The flower turns upright after pollination, explaining the genus name, *Monotropa* (one turn).

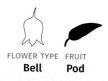

FLOWER TYPE   FRUIT
Bell   **Pod**

Arrowhead
Sagittaria latifolia

Family: Water-Plantain (Alismataceae)

Height: aquatic

Flower: white flowers, ½–1" (1–2.5 cm) wide, in whorls of 3 sit on an erect stalk; each flower has 3 oval white-to-green petals around the center

Leaf: large, toothless, arrowhead-shaped leaves, 5–16" (12.5–40 cm) long, with strong veins; each leaf is held above the water on its own stalk; stems arise from base of plant

Bloom: summer, fall

Cycle/Origin: perennial, native

Habitat: an aquatic plant of wet areas, found along slow-moving streams, ponds and quiet lakes

Range: throughout

Stan's Notes: Over ten species of Arrowhead are found in the U.S., six of which occur in Michigan, with this being the most common. The leaves can be extremely narrow or very wide. It grows in the muddy bottoms of calm waters and produces edible tubers eaten by muskrats, swans, geese and ducks, hence its other common name, Duck Potatoes. These tubers, also called wapatoo, have long been gathered by people for food. Leaves are held above the water surface, unlike the floating leaves of the White Water Lily (pg. 321). A favorite food of migrating Tundra Swans and also eaten by Trumpeter Swans.

FLOWER TYPE
Regular

LEAF TYPE
Simple Lobed

LEAF ATTACHMENT
Basal

Black Snakeroot
Sanicula marilandica

Family: Parsley (Apiaceae)

Height: 1–4' (30–120 cm)

Flower: 3–5 round clusters of white-to-cream flowers, each ½–1" (1–2.5 cm) in diameter, sit on the end of thin stalks

Leaf: a large leaf, 3–5" (7.5–12.5 cm) wide, with 3–5 leaflets, each of which has 3 lobes; leaf edges have alternating large and small teeth

Bloom: summer

Cycle/Origin: perennial, native

Habitat: dry woods, along forest edges

Range: throughout

Stan's Notes: A very common plant of forests throughout Michigan, the Black Snakeroot's small flowers produce small oval seeds covered with tiny hairs and bristles, allowing the seeds to spread by "hitchhiking" in the fur of animals. Like all plants of the Parsley family, it has flat or round clusters of flowers. This wildflower is one of many different plants with the common name "Snakeroot," and one of several very similar species that occur in Michigan. Its genus name, *Sanicula*, comes from the Latin *sanare*, or "to heal," as it was once thought that this group of plants harbored healing powers.

CLUSTER TYPE
Round

LEAF TYPE
Palmate

LEAF ATTACHMENT
Alternate

LEAF ATTACHMENT
Clasping

False Lily-of-the-Valley
Maianthemum canadense

Family: Asparagus (Asparagaceae)

Height: 2–6" (5–15 cm)

Flower: small spike cluster of white flowers on a stalk, ½–3" (1–7.5 cm) tall; individual flowers, ⅙" (.5 cm) wide, are star-shaped; 2 petals and 2 petal-like sepals give the appearance of 4 petals

Leaf: 2 (occasionally 3) pointed, lance-shaped leaves alternate along a zigzag stem; stalkless leaves

Fruit: green berries turn dull red with dull white speckles

Bloom: spring

Cycle/Origin: perennial, native

Habitat: shade, coniferous woods, deciduous woods

Range: throughout

Stan's Notes: Also called Wild Lily-of-the-Valley or Canada Mayflower, this low plant of coniferous and deciduous forests can be found throughout the state. Its stem is often zigzagged, going back and forth between alternating leaves. It grows in large mats connected by an underground root system (rhizome).

CLUSTER TYPE	FLOWER TYPE	LEAF TYPE	LEAF ATTACHMENT	FRUIT
Spike	Regular	Simple	Alternate	Berry

fruit

Wild Strawberry
Fragaria virginiana

Family: Rose (Roseaceae)

Height: 3–6" (7.5–15 cm)

Flower: 2–10 white flowers, ¾" (2 cm) wide; each flower has 5 round petals surrounding a yellow center

Leaf: each 3-part basal leaf, 3" (7.5 cm) wide, sits on a long hairy stalk; each leaflet, 1" (2.5 cm) long, is coarsely toothed

Fruit: bright red berry

Bloom: spring

Cycle/Origin: perennial, native

Habitat: dry, sun, edges of woods

Range: throughout

Stan's Notes: Often growing in large patches, Wild Strawberry produces some of the sweetest tasting wild berries. A parent species from which cultivated strawberries are derived. One of several species of strawberry in Michigan, it is common just about anywhere in the state. Flowers and fruit are always on stems separate from the leaves.

FLOWER TYPE
Regular

LEAF TYPE
Compound

LEAF ATTACHMENT
Basal

FRUIT
Berry

Dutchman's Breeches

Dicentra cucullaria

Family: Poppy (Papaveraceae)

Height: 4–12" (10–30 cm)

Flower: a collection of waxy flowers, unusually shaped, ¾" (2 cm) long, white-to-pink with yellow tips; each flower is made up of 4 petals and 2 large inflated tubes (spurs) that appear like upside-down pants

Leaf: greenish gray leaves, paler in color beneath and deeply divided, arise from the base of the plant; each leaf has a soft feathery appearance

Fruit: oblong pod-like container that opens at the base

Bloom: spring

Cycle/Origin: perennial, native

Habitat: deciduous woods

Range: throughout

Stan's Notes: A spring ephemeral, Dutchman's Breeches blooms and sets seed each spring before the trees above it have a chance to sprout leaves. Its genus name, *Dicentra*, is derived from the Greek word for "two-spurred," and refers to its long inflated flower spurs that contain the nectar. Only spring bumblebees with a mouth part (proboscis) long enough to delve deep into the flower can sip nectar from its flowers. Some insects have developed a way around this long tube and "cheat" by chewing a hole in the spur to access the nectar.

CLUSTER TYPE
Spike

FLOWER TYPE
Irregular

LEAF TYPE
Compound

LEAF ATTACHMENT
Basal

FRUIT
Pod

Canada Violet
Viola canadensis

Family: Violet (Violaceae)

Height: 8–16" (20–40 cm)

Flower: white, typically violet-shaped flower, ¾–1" (2–2.5 cm) wide, with a yellow center, sits on a slender, purplish stalk; flowers stand above the leaves and are often tinged pink with age

Leaf: thin purplish stalks with sparse hairs hold wide heart-shaped leaves, 1–3" (2.5–7.5 cm) wide, lacking teeth

Bloom: spring, summer

Cycle/Origin: perennial, native

Habitat: wet, cool, shade, rich deciduous woods

Range: throughout

Stan's Notes: One of the few "stalked" violets, the Canada Violet's flowers rise from a stalk rather than the more typical single basal flower stalk arrangement of most violets. It grows in patches from aboveground runners (stolons) and is one of the few violets that emits a fragrance. Once established, Canada Violet grows well as a garden plant. A good plant for a shady part of your yard or garden.

FLOWER TYPE **Irregular** LEAF TYPE **Simple** LEAF ATTACHMENT **Alternate**

fruit

Bluebead Lily
Clintonia borealis

Family: Lily (Liliaceae)

Height: 6–10" (15–25 cm)

Flower: 3–6 creamy, yellow-to-white, slightly drooping flowers per stalk, each approximately ¾–1" (2–2.5 cm) long, and made up of 6 petals (3 petals and 3 petal-like sepals)

Leaf: 2–4 simple, lance-shaped, toothless leaves, 5–8" (12.5–20 cm) long; thick and fleshy

Fruit: numerous shiny, blue-to-black oval berries, ½" (1 cm)

Bloom: spring

Cycle/Origin: perennial, native

Habitat: damp woods, mostly coniferous

Range: throughout, except for lower third of the L.P.

Stan's Notes: Also called Yellow Clintonia due to its yellowish flowers, the Bluebead Lily has poisonous berries, proving that not all blue berries are edible. Its leaves are thick and fleshy, ooze clear fluids when broken, and smell like cucumbers when crushed. Look closely for silky white hairs along the leaves' edges (margins). The name of this very common plant of northern Michigan honors the late New York governor DeWitt Clinton (1769–1828).

FLOWER TYPE **Regular**   LEAF TYPE **Simple**   LEAF ATTACHMENT **Basal**   FRUIT **Berry**

White Clover

Trifolium repens

Family: Pea or Bean (Fabaceae)

Height: 4–10" (10–25 cm)

Flower: white (tinged with pink), fragrant, pea-like, irregular flowers, ¼" (.6 cm) wide, form round cluster, 1" (2.5 cm) wide, on a single long stalk

Leaf: 3 leaflets grow on a long basal stalk to form a compound leaf, 1½" (4 cm) wide; individual leaflets, ¼–½" (.6–1 cm) wide, are round with fine teeth and have a characteristic, dusty white, triangular marking

Bloom: spring, summer, fall

Cycle/Origin: perennial, non-native

Habitat: dry, sun, lawns, fields

Range: throughout

Stan's Notes: Well known for occasionally producing a four-leaf clover, White Clover is a Eurasian import that has found a comfortable home in lawns across North America. It spreads by an aboveground stem that roots at each leaf attachment (node). The genus name, *Trifolium*, describes its three leaflets, while the species name, *repens*, refers to its "creeping" habit of growth. Look for the dusty white triangular markings on its leaves to help you identify this sometimes "lucky" plant. White clover is very attractive to a number of butterfly species including skippers, blues, sulphurs and hairstreaks.

CLUSTER TYPE
Round

FLOWER TYPE
Irregular

LEAF ATTACHMENT
Alternate

LEAF TYPE
Compound

Bouncing Bet
Saponaria officinalis

Family: Pink (Caryophyllaceae)

Height: 1–2' (30–60 cm)

Flower: several white-to-pink flowers, 1" (2.5 cm) wide, loosely arranged at the top of a single stem; each flower has 5 ragged-tipped petals

Leaf: narrow opposite leaves, 2–3" (5–7.5 cm) long and ½" (1 cm) wide, with 3–5 conspicuous veins

Bloom: summer, fall

Cycle/Origin: perennial, non-native

Habitat: roadsides, ditches, disturbed soils

Range: throughout

Stan's Notes: Often seen growing in patches along roadsides. Its white flowers are often pink and look similar to phlox. Also called Soapwort because its roots contain saponin, a chemical that becomes slippery and sudsy when wet. It was once used as a soap. Spreads by underground roots (rhizomes), but also produces large amounts of small black seeds. Makes a good garden plant, but will spread.

CLUSTER TYPE
Round

FLOWER TYPE
Regular

LEAF TYPE
Simple

LEAF ATTACHMENT
Opposite

Indian Hemp
Apocynum cannabinum

Family: Dogbane (Apocynaceae)

Height: 1–3' (30–90 cm)

Flower: a round cluster, 1" (2.5 cm) wide, of 2–10 tiny, whitish green flowers, each ⅓" (.8 cm) wide with 5 petals, found at the end of an erect stalk

Leaf: oval-shaped, toothless leaves, often have a wavy edge (margin)

Fruit: long, thin pod-like capsules, 3–8" (7.5–20 cm), that open along one side, revealing seeds attached to long tufts of white fuzz that help carry them on the wind

Bloom: summer

Cycle/Origin: perennial, native

Habitat: moist, sun, along roads, deciduous woods

Range: throughout

Stan's Notes: Indian Hemp is a tall perennial plant with a single main stem that branches out into many spreading stems. A close relative of the milkweeds, it produces a thick, white milky juice in its stem and leaves; this juice contains cardiac glycosides that cause hot flashes, rapid heartbeat and fatigue. Insects avoid this plant because of the poisonous juice. Like Spreading Dogbane (pg. 101), its close relative, Indian Hemp's long stems, when dried and peeled, make a strong cord once used by Native Americans, hence its common name. Fibrous stems of old plants are often used by orioles to construct nests.

CLUSTER TYPE	FLOWER TYPE	LEAF TYPE	LEAF ATTACHMENT	FRUIT
Round	**Regular**	**Simple**	**Opposite**	**Pod**

Rue Anemone
Thalictrum thalictroides

Family: Buttercup (Ranunculaceae)

Height: 4–8" (10–20 cm)

Flower: 2–3 white-to-pink (or lavender) flowers with a green center made up of 5–10 petal-like sepals, 1" (2.5 cm) wide

Leaf: leaves appear to be simple lobed, but are actually 5–8 compound leaves, each composed of 3 leaflets, 1" (2.5 cm) long; each leaflet has 3 rounded tips; leaves whorled just below the flowers

Bloom: spring

Cycle/Origin: perennial, native

Habitat: wet, deciduous woods

Range: southern half of the L.P.

Stan's Notes: A woodland early spring bloomer, Rue Anemone usually grows in large groups, carpeting the forest floor. At about 3–4" (7.5–10 cm) from the ground, its single stem branches into many stems and flower stalks, supporting leaves and a total of two to five flowers, one flower per stalk. Its flower color ranges widely from white to pink to lavender. While its leaves are similar to anemones, this plant is not a true anemone. Its flowers lack nectar, attracting insects instead by the color and shape of the flower. It reproduces mainly by underground roots. Its common name "Rue" comes from the similarity of its leaves to those of the meadow rues (pp. 79 and 315).

FLOWER TYPE
Regular

LEAF TYPE
Compound

LEAF ATTACHMENT
Whorl

Wood Anemone
Anemone quinquefolia

Family: Buttercup (Ranunculaceae)

Height: 4–8" (10–20 cm)

Flower: a single white flower, 1" (2.5 cm) wide, rises above the leaves; each flower has 5 petal-like white sepals (sepals can be pink or rarely purple)

Leaf: a set of whorled leaves; each individual leaf has 3–5 coarse-toothed and pointed lobes, 1¼" (3 cm) long

Bloom: spring

Cycle/Origin: perennial, native

Habitat: dry, shade, openings and edges of deciduous woods

Range: throughout

Stan's Notes: Also called Mayflower, Wood Anemone is a common spring wildflower (it flowers before the trees above have a chance to set leaves). While its flowers are usually white, they are sometimes pink. It reproduces along a horizontal underground rootstock (rhizome) to form large mats or patches of growth. The genus name, *Anemone*, comes from the Greek word for "wind," and refers to the plant's thin stalk, which trembles in the wind. Plants that bloom are older than non-bloomers. It may take five years or more to reach flowering age.

FLOWER TYPE
Regular

LEAF TYPE
Simple Lobed

LEAF ATTACHMENT
Whorl

237

White Trout Lily
Erythronium albidum

Family: Lily (Liliaceae)

Height: 5–10" (12.5–25 cm)

Flower: each stalk produces a single hanging white flower, 1" (2.5 cm) wide; each flower has a yellow center, sometimes tinted with violet on the back, and 6 backward-curving petals that are actually 3 petals and 3 petal-like sepals

Leaf: a pair of elliptical, pointed basal leaves, up to 8" (20 cm) long, with brownish purple spots and streaks

Fruit: egg-shaped pod-like container

Bloom: spring

Cycle/Origin: perennial, native

Habitat: dry, deciduous woods

Range: southern half of the L.P.

Stan's Notes: Also called Dogtooth Violet, White Trout Lily is a member of the Lily family, not a violet. The common name "Trout" comes from its mottled leaves, which resemble the coloring of a Brown Trout. One of the most common spring wildflowers found carpeting deciduous forest floors, the White Trout Lily reproduces mostly by underground bulbs. Nearly identical to the Yellow Trout Lily (pg. 361), except for the color of the flower.

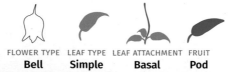

FLOWER TYPE **Bell**   LEAF TYPE **Simple**   LEAF ATTACHMENT **Basal**   FRUIT **Pod**

White Campion
Silene latifolia

Family: Pink (Caryophyllaceae)

Height: 1–3' (30–90 cm)

Flower: many white flowers, 1" (2.5 cm) wide, each with 5 deeply notched petals, giving the appearance of 10 petals; large, dark-veined, green "bladders" (calyx) behind each flower

Leaf: hairy lance-shaped leaves, 1–4" (2.5–10 cm) long

Fruit: brown, vase-shaped capsule ½" (1 cm) long

Bloom: summer

Cycle/Origin: annual, non-native

Habitat: dry, fields, gardens, along roads, disturbed soils

Range: throughout

Stan's Notes: An evening-blooming plant, White Campion's many white flowers are easy to see at night and attract night-flying insects, such as moths. Its male and female flowers are found on separate plants (called dioecious), and its petals retract back into each flower's sticky "bladder" during the day. A European import, it often pops up in untended gardens, and along roads and open fields. Also called Bladder Campion or Evening Lychnis. This plant grows among other plants, and its many branches, stems and joints give it a bushy appearance. Seeds shake out of its capsule on the winter winds. Good food for finches and sparrows.

FLOWER TYPE
Regular

LEAF TYPE
Simple

LEAF ATTACHMENT
Opposite

FRUIT
Pod

Hoary Alyssum
Berteroa incana

Family: Mustard (Brassicaceae)

Height: 1–3' (30–90 cm)

Flower: spike cluster, 1" (2.5 cm) tall, of tiny white flowers, ¼" (.6 cm), each consisting of 4 petals; each petal is partly divided (notched) so each flower looks like it is made up of 8 petals

Leaf: thin lance-shaped leaves, ½" (1 cm) long, covered with pale white hairs, giving them a downy appearance; leaves alternate along a single stem that divides near the top

Fruit: many small, round, pointed, pod-like containers, ¼" (.6 cm) long, covered with downy hair

Bloom: summer, fall

Cycle/Origin: annual, non-native

Habitat: dry, sun, open fields, along roads, disturbed sites

Range: throughout

Stan's Notes: The Hoary Alyssum usually appears as a single-stemmed erect plant that branches only near the top to accommodate spike clusters of small white flowers. The entire plant is covered with gray-to-white hair, hence the common name, "Hoary." Its flowers have four petals, indicating a member of the Mustard family. A European import, two species of alyssum grow in North America. A host plant for Cabbage butterfly caterpillars.

CLUSTER TYPE	FLOWER TYPE	LEAF TYPE	LEAF ATTACHMENT	FRUIT
Spike	**Regular**	**Simple**	**Alternate**	**Pod**

243

Thimbleweed
Anemone virginiana

Family: Buttercup (Ranunculaceae)

Height: 2–3' (60–90 cm)

Flower: thimble-shaped center of flower, 1" (2.5 cm) tall, is about twice as long as it is wide; 5 white petal-like sepals, ¾" (2 cm) long; each flower is on a single, long, thin stalk

Leaf: basal leaves are divided into 3 coarsely toothed lobes, 3" (7.5 cm) long; leaves on the stem (cauline) are similar but smaller and are whorled around the stem

Bloom: summer

Cycle/Origin: perennial, native

Habitat: dry, sun, rocky outcroppings, open woods

Range: throughout

Stan's Notes: Also called the Virginia Thimbleweed. One of a number of species of *Anemone* in Michigan, the Thimbleweed is a single-stemmed plant with two to three sets of whorled leaves (each group of whorled leaves has two, three or five leaves). The length of the flower's center, or "thimble," differentiates the Thimbleweed from the Long-fruited Thimbleweed (pg. 293). Like some members of the Buttercup family, its flower lacks petals, and instead has large petal-like sepals. Thimble-shaped seed heads turn cottony with many small seeds in autumn.

FLOWER TYPE
Regular

LEAF TYPE
Simple Lobed

LEAF ATTACHMENT
Basal

LEAF ATTACHMENT
Whorl

fruit

Bearberry

Arctostaphylos uva-ursi

Family: Heath (Ericaceae)

Height: 6–12" (15–30 cm)

Flower: a round cluster, 1" (2.5 cm) wide, of white-to-pink, bell-shaped flowers; individual flowers, ¼" (.6 cm) long, are waxy white bell flowers tinged with pink at the narrow flower opening

Leaf: oval-shaped, smooth, leathery leaves without teeth attach alternately along the creeping woody stem

Fruit: cluster of bright red berries

Bloom: spring, summer

Cycle/Origin: perennial, native

Habitat: dry, sun, exposed rocky sites in coniferous forests

Range: throughout, except for the southeastern L.P.

Stan's Notes: A woody shrub, appearing more like herbaceous ground cover, Bearberry's woody stems are usually hidden under moss or leaf litter. The woody stems have a papery bark that sloughs off (exfoliates). Often forms large mats. The red berries are eaten by many birds and especially bears. The genus name comes from the Greek *arctos* (bear) and *staphyle* (bunch of grapes), describing the fruit.

CLUSTER TYPE
Round

FLOWER TYPE
Bell

LEAF TYPE
Simple

LEAF ATTACHMENT
Alternate

FRUIT
Berry

Pussytoes
Antennaria neglecta

Family: Aster (Asteraceae)

Height: 4–12" (10–30 cm)

Flower: a 1" (2.5 cm) round cluster of 3–10 white, fuzzy flowers, ¼" (.6 cm) long, on top of a single fuzzy stem

Leaf: spoon-shaped, single-veined basal leaves, 1–2" (2.5–5 cm) long, are covered in white hairs, with a fuzzy appearance; leaves on the stems are very small, ¼" (.6 cm) long, and often go unnoticed

Bloom: spring

Cycle/Origin: perennial, native

Habitat: dry, sun or shade, open woods, rocky outcroppings

Range: southern half of the L.P.

Stan's Notes: Although its flowers are white, its dense covering of hairs make Pussytoes appear to be gray. The bristly flower heads resemble a cat's paw, hence the common name. Other species of Pussytoes are slightly taller and have between three to five veins on the basal leaves as opposed to the single vein of this plant. Often grows to form a dense mat. It can be very difficult to correctly identify this plant. This plant is so variable that even botanists don't agree on the number of species or where the species are found. This is an allelopathic plant, giving off chemicals that "poison" the soil for other plants, reducing competition for moisture and sunlight.

CLUSTER TYPE **Round** FLOWER TYPE **Composite** LEAF TYPE **Simple** LEAF ATTACHMENT **Basal**

249

Canada Anemone
Anemone canadensis

Family: Buttercup (Ranunculaceae)

Height: 1–2' (30–60 cm)

Flower: a regular flower, 1–1½" (2.5–4 cm) wide, with 5 white petal-like sepals and a yellow center; each flower sits on a single, long, hairy stalk

Leaf: long-stalked, coarsely toothed basal leaves are deeply divided into 3 narrow segments; leaves on the stalk (cauline) are coarsely toothed, stalkless, whorled, deeply lobed and usually divided into 3 parts

Bloom: spring, summer

Cycle/Origin: perennial, native

Habitat: wet meadows, prairies

Range: throughout

Stan's Notes: Also called the Canada Windflower or Meadow Anemone, the Canada Anemone is a perennial that spreads by horizontal underground roots (rhizomes), which often cause it to grow in large patches. Its flowers are actually the yellow center, while the white petals are modified leaves (sepals). Over 80 species of *Anemone* can be found throughout the world, about 25 species in North America alone, some of which are grown as garden flowers. All have a whorl of leaves on the stalk (cauline) just below the flower.

FLOWER TYPE
Regular

LEAF TYPE
Simple Lobed

LEAF ATTACHMENT
Basal

LEAF ATTACHMENT
Whorl

Nodding Trillium

Trillium cernuum

Family: Bunchflower (Melanthiaceae)

Height: 6–24" (15–60 cm)

Flower: a single white flower, 1–1½" (2.5–4 cm) wide, made up of 3 white petals and 3 green sepals; flowers hang below a whorl of leaves on a short stalk, 1–2" (2.5–5 cm) long

Leaf: a single whorl of 3 wavy-edged, toothless and stalkless diamond-shaped leaves with pointed tips

Fruit: a single red-to-purple berry

Bloom: spring, summer

Cycle/Origin: perennial, native

Habitat: wet, shade, deciduous woods

Range: throughout

Stan's Notes: Nodding Trillium is one of nine species of trillium in Michigan, all of which are protected by conservation laws. The species name *cernuum* comes from the Latin word for "drooping" or "nodding," and refers to the flower position. Its leaves are often confused with that of the Jack-in-the-pulpit (pg. 81). If any part of the plant is picked, the leaves may not be able to produce enough starch and sugar to replenish the bulb to bloom the next year, thus killing the plant. Enjoy in the wild only!

FLOWER TYPE
Regular

LEAF TYPE
Simple

LEAF ATTACHMENT
Whorl

FRUIT
Berry

fruit

Bunchberry
Cornus canadensis

Family: Dogwood (Cornaceae)

Height: 3–8" (7.5–20 cm)

Flower: 4 white, petal-like bracts, 1½" (4 cm) long, surround a group of tiny green flowers, ⅛" (.3 cm) wide, giving the appearance of a single, large, white flower

Leaf: 4–6 toothless, elliptical leaves with pointed ends and deep curving veins, whorling around a central woody stem

Fruit: tight bunch of bright red berries

Bloom: spring

Cycle/Origin: perennial, native

Habitat: coniferous forest floor

Range: throughout, except for the southeastern L.P.

Stan's Notes: Underground stems (rhizomes) spread this smallest member of the Dogwood family in large patches on the forest floor. Each leaf vein runs independently to the leaf's edge. Look for tiny scale-like leaves on the stem just below the whorl of main leaves. A common plant of Northern Michigan, the Bunchberry is related to the Red-twigged Dogwood, a common ornamental shrub. A host plant for Spring Azure butterfly caterpillars.

FLOWER TYPE
Regular

LEAF TYPE
Simple

LEAF ATTACHMENT
Whorl

FRUIT
Berry

255

Bloodroot

Sanguinaria canadensis

Family: Poppy (Papaveraceae)

Height: 5–10" (12.5–25 cm)

Flower: large, single, white (sometimes pink) flowers, 1½" (4 cm) wide, each with 8–10 petals and a golden yellow center; each flower on its own pinkish stalk

Leaf: large, bluish green, round leaves, 4–7" (10–18 cm) wide, 5–9 lobes per leaf, sit on a long leafstalk; leaves wrap around flower stalk, opening horizontally (flat) after bloom

Fruit: pod-like capsule splits to reveal many brown seeds

Bloom: spring

Cycle/Origin: perennial, native

Habitat: deciduous woods

Range: throughout

Stan's Notes: These flowers lack nectar, quickly dropping petals after pollination, leaving a large, pointed pod-like capsule. One of the earliest plants, it emerges from nearly frozen soil, flowering well before trees leaf out. Its flowers open on sunny days, closing tightly at night. Leaves unroll in full sun, curling up around the flower stalk at night and on cloudy days. The genus name, *Sanguinaria*, comes from Latin word for "bleeding," describing the red-orange juice in the stems and roots, used by many cultures as a dye and insect repellent. Easy to grow in gardens; don't dig it from the wild.

FLOWER TYPE
Regular

LEAF TYPE
Simple Lobed

LEAF ATTACHMENT
Basal

FRUIT
Pod

Trailing Arbutus
Epigaea repens

Family: Heath (Ericaceae)

Height: 1–4" (2.5–10 cm)

Flower: a tight round cluster, 1–2" (2.5–5 cm) wide, of many white-to-pink flowers; individual flowers, ¼–½" (.6–1 cm) wide, have 5 flaring petals clustered near the ground, often under the leaves

Leaf: oval, olive green, leathery leaves, 1–3" (2.5–7.5 cm) long, alternate along the trailing woody stem; tiny hairs along the leaf edge (margin)

Fruit: brown pod-like container with 5 segments

Bloom: spring

Cycle/Origin: perennial, native

Habitat: dry, sandy soils, coniferous woods

Range: throughout, except for the southeastern L.P.

Stan's Notes: A common, trailing (creeping) wildflower with white (rarely pink) and very fragrant flowers, the Trailing Arbutus is an early bloomer. Five petals fuse at their bases to form a short tube. The leaves and, to a lesser extent, the flowers are often hidden beneath the leaves and needles of other plants. The stems, along with the leaf edges, are covered by stiff rusty brown hairs. Not as common as it once was, it seems to be a victim of logging and other disturbances.

CLUSTER TYPE
Round

FLOWER TYPE
Regular

LEAF TYPE
Simple

LEAF ATTACHMENT
Alternate

FRUIT
Pod

259

fruit

Thimbleberry
Rubus parviflorus

Family: Rose (Roseaceae)

Height: 3–6' (90–180 cm)

Flower: single white flower per stem, 1–2" (2.5–5 cm) wide, with 5 petals and numerous yellow flower parts in the center; can have numerous flowers at the same time

Leaf: 5-lobed maple-shaped leaf, 4–8" (10–20 cm) long, with numerous sharp teeth and deep veins; each leaf attached alternately along the stems

Fruit: single reddish berry that resembles a very large raspberry

Bloom: spring, summer

Cycle/Origin: perennial, native

Habitat: woodland edges

Range: throughout

Stan's Notes: A woody shrub that often grows along edges of woodland, where there is enough sunlight to survive. The large showy flowers produce raspberry-like fruit big enough to fit over a finger, like a sewing thimble, hence the common name. The fruit is edible and excellent for making jam or eating directly off the plant.

FLOWER TYPE
Regular

LEAF TYPE
Simple Lobed

LEAF ATTACHMENT
Alternate

FRUIT
Berry

fruit

Mayapple
Podophyllum peltatum

Family: Barberry (Berberidaceae)

Height: 12–18" (30–45 cm)

Flower: single, nodding, waxy white flower with 6–9 petals, 1–2" (2.5–5 cm) wide; each flower is on a thin ascending stalk rising from a crotch between the 2 leaves

Leaf: set of 2 deeply lobed leaves, 12–15" (30–37.5 cm) across; each leaf has up to 5 lobes and stands well above the flower

Bloom: spring

Cycle/Origin: perennial, native

Habitat: wet, moist woods, shady meadows

Range: southern half of the L.P.

Stan's Notes: A spring flowering plant of rich woods and shady clearings, sometimes called the Mandrake. Its common name "Mayapple" refers to the blooming time. Its other common name comes from the mistaken belief that the Mayapple's roots appear similar to the roots of the Mandrake, a European plant. The leaves, stems and roots are toxic. However, in summer the large lemon-shaped berries are edible. The blooming of this plant has been used as an indicator of when to start looking for the elusive morel mushroom.

FLOWER TYPE
Regular

LEAF TYPE
Simple Lobed

LEAF ATTACHMENT
Opposite

FRUIT
Pod

FRUIT
Berry

fruit

Bur Cucumber
Sicyos angulatus

Family: Gourd (Cucurbitaceae)

Height: 2–10' (60–300 cm); climbing vine

Flower: a round cluster, 1–2" (2.5–5 cm) wide, of small white flowers, ½" (1 cm) wide, each with 5 pointed petals; the flowering stalk arises from a leaf joint (axis)

Leaf: large maple-like leaves, 4–6" (10–15 cm) wide, each with 5 lobes

Fruit: cluster of up to 10 small pod-like containers, ½–1" (1–2.5 cm) round, each covered with tiny rubbery spines; each pod contains a single seed

Bloom: summer, fall

Cycle/Origin: annual, native

Habitat: wet, shade, deciduous woods, along streams, lakes and wetlands

Range: southern half of the L.P.

Stan's Notes: The Bur Cucumber looks very similar to the Wild Cucumber (pg. 323), but grows in drier areas. The Bur Cucumber has long, curly forked tendrils and a hairy stem. Its leaves, flower stalks and tendrils all arise from the same location on the vine.

CLUSTER TYPE
Round

FLOWER TYPE
Regular

LEAF TYPE
Simple Lobed

LEAF ATTACHMENT
Alternate

FRUIT
Pod

Whorled Milkweed

Asclepias verticillata

Family: Dogbane (Apocynaceae)

Height: 6–15" (15–37.5 cm)

Flower: tiny white flowers, ⅛" (.3 cm) wide, form a flat cluster, 1–2" (2.5–5 cm) wide; individual flowers have 5 downward-curving petals and 5 upward-pointing petals, referred to as a crown

Leaf: 3–6 whorled, very narrow needle-like leaves, 1–2" (2.5–5 cm) long

Bloom: summer

Cycle/Origin: perennial, native

Habitat: dry, sun, prairies, rocky soils, along roads

Range: southern half of the L.P.

Stan's Notes: Whorled Milkweed usually has one thin stem that branches near the top into several flat-topped flower clusters. Each flower has a slit that allows an insect's legs to slip inside and emerge with a pair of pollen sacs so the insect can unwittingly pollinate another flower. This complicated process means that only a few flowers become pollinated. Whorled Milkweed often grows in patches in nutrient-poor soils, and like many other milkweeds, it has been used in folk medicine. In fact, its genus name, *Asclepias*, is in honor of Aesculapius, the Greek god of medicine. One of the first plants to come back after prairie fires. Visited by solitary bees and ants for nectar.

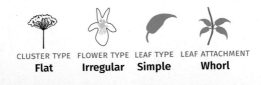

CLUSTER TYPE **Flat**   FLOWER TYPE **Irregular**   LEAF TYPE **Simple**   LEAF ATTACHMENT **Whorl**

White Snakeroot
Ageratina altissima

Family: Aster (Asteraceae)

Height: 1–3' (30–90 cm)

Flower: many tiny, white flowers, ⅛" (.5 cm) wide, form several flat clusters, 1–2" (2.5–5 cm) wide

Leaf: dark green leaves, 2–6" (5–15 cm) long, widest at leaf base with a pointed end and ragged teeth

Bloom: fall

Cycle/Origin: perennial, native

Habitat: dry, shade, edges of deciduous woods

Range: southern half of the L.P. and the western U.P.

Stan's Notes: Well known as a fall-blooming wildflower, White Snakeroot grows along the shady edges of deciduous woods. The plant contains a toxic chemical that when ingested by a cow causes milk sickness. If humans subsequently drink milk produced by that cow, they will also suffer from the disease, which killed Abraham Lincoln's mother. Today, because of better food availability for cows and modern processing, this is no longer a health concern. Many plants share "Snake" in the common name because of the belief that plants growing in the shade harbor snakes or that the plant might be used for treatment of snakebite. Like other members of the Aster family, the White Snakeroot has composite flowers composed entirely of disk flowers, lacking ray flowers.

CLUSTER TYPE
Flat

FLOWER TYPE
Composite

LEAF TYPE
Simple

LEAF ATTACHMENT
Opposite

269

seeds

Pennycress
Thlaspi arvense

Family: Mustard (Brassicaceae)

Height: 5–18" (12.5–45 cm)

Flower: small white flowers, ¼" (.6 cm) wide, that grow in short spike clusters, 1–2" (2.5–5 cm) long; individual flowers have 4 petals that form a cross shape

Leaf: stalkless, coarsely toothed, lance-shaped leaves, 2–4" (5–10 cm) long

Fruit: flat, round, notched pod-like containers that look like paper pennies

Bloom: spring

Cycle/Origin: annual, non-native

Habitat: dry, sun, disturbed soils, along roads

Range: throughout

Stan's Notes: The Pennycress is a common annual of disturbed soils, and is often found in farmyards, schoolyards and along trails and roads. Its flowers bloom from the bottom up, and each flower produces a characteristic flat "penny" pod with a large notch on the top. Like all members of the Mustard family, its four flower petals form a cross shape, which helps to identify the plant. Its seed pods turn brown and papery, and its black seeds are hot and peppery and have been used as a pepper substitute. This native of Europe is also called Field Pennycress.

CLUSTER TYPE	FLOWER TYPE	LEAF TYPE	LEAF ATTACHMENT	FRUIT
Spike	**Regular**	**Simple**	**Alternate**	**Pod**

Pearly Everlasting
Anaphalis margaritacea

Family: Aster (Asteraceae)

Height: 1–3' (30–90 cm)

Flower: a round cluster, 1–2" (2.5–5 cm) wide, made of many individual, white flower heads; individual flowers, ¼" (.6 cm) tall, are composed of white, petal-like bracts surrounding a yellow center (disk flowers)

Leaf: long, narrow, greenish white leaves, 3–5" (7.5–12.5 cm), alternate along the stem; leaves are densely hairy underneath, causing them to look woolly white

Bloom: summer, fall

Cycle/Origin: perennial, native

Habitat: dry, sun, pastures, along roads, fields

Range: throughout

Stan's Notes: A common plant of Michigan, Pearly Everlasting blooms from summer to autumn. Its stems are covered with soft cottony hairs, and its flower clusters are often dried and used in floral arrangements. While it is the only species of its genus found in North America, individual plants can be highly variable. A host plant for American Painted Lady butterfly caterpillars; the adults overwinter as adults but often don't survive. The region is re-colonized by adults from more-southern locations each year.

CLUSTER TYPE
Round

FLOWER TYPE
Composite

LEAF TYPE
Simple

LEAF ATTACHMENT
Alternate

273

Field Bindweed
Convolvulus arvensis

Family: Morning Glory (Convolvulaceae)

Height: 1–6' (30–180 cm); climbing vine

Flower: white, tube or funnel-shaped flowers, 1–2" (2.5–5 cm) wide; 5 petals fuse together to form the flower

Leaf: small, triangular or arrowhead-shaped, toothless leaves, 1–2" (2.5–5 cm) long, alternate along the climbing, twisting stem

Bloom: summer, fall

Growth: perennial, non-native

Habitat: dry, sunny fields, usually creeping along the ground but occasionally climbing on fences or shrubs

Range: throughout the L.P.

Stan's Notes: Very similar to Hedge Bindweed (pg. 297), this wildflower of summer is usually so small that it goes unnoticed until its pure white flowers open on sunny days. Closely related to the Common Blue Morning Glory of the garden, the Field Bindweed seems to prefer disturbed soils, old fields, abandoned lots in cities, and suburban lawns. It grows in large tangled mats, and its flowers are sometimes slightly pink. The genus name, *Convolvulus*, is from the Latin *convolvere*, meaning "to entwine," which accurately describes its growing habit. Lacking tendrils to grasp other plants, it twists its stems around host plants for support, seeking sunlight, a habit that provides its other common name, Possession Vine.

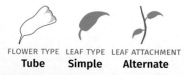

FLOWER TYPE **Tube** LEAF TYPE **Simple** LEAF ATTACHMENT **Alternate**

Ox-eye Daisy
Leucanthemum vulgare

Family: Aster (Asteraceae)

Height: 1–3' (30–90 cm)

Flower: a common white-and-yellow flower head, 1–2" (2.5–5 cm) wide, with up to 20 white petals (ray flowers) surrounding a yellow center of disk flowers

Leaf: dandelion-like, lobed, thick, dark green, clasping basal leaves, up to 6" (15 cm) long; stem leaves, 1–2" (2.5–5 cm) long, similar to basal leaves, only smaller

Bloom: spring, summer

Cycle/Origin: perennial, non-native

Habitat: wet or dry, sun, fields, along roads, pastures

Range: throughout

Stan's Notes: Also called the Common Daisy, the Ox-eye Daisy is a European import often seen growing in patches along roads. In poor soil it grows short and erect; in rich soils it grows tall, and its weak stem causes it to fall over and spread out across the ground. Ox-eye Daisy contains pyrethrum, a chemical that repels insects and is used in organic pesticides. This nice garden plant is often overlooked. A very interesting composite of many flowers appearing as one large flower. Each white petal is a separate flower, while the center yellow portion is many individual disk flowers.

FLOWER TYPE
Composite

LEAF TYPE
Simple Lobed

LEAF ATTACHMENT
Alternate

LEAF ATTACHMENT
Basal

LEAF ATTACHMENT
Clasping

Star-flowered Solomon's Seal
Maianthemum stellatum

Family: Asparagus (Asparagaceae)

Height: 1–2' (30–60 cm)

Flower: spike cluster, 1–3" (2.5–7.5 cm) long, of creamy white star-shaped flowers, ¼" (.6 cm) wide, that cluster at the end of the single stem

Leaf: folded, sometimes trough-like, lance-shaped leaves, 2–6" (5–15 cm) long, lacking teeth, with parallel veins, alternately clasping the zigzag stem

Fruit: green and red berries with obvious dark bands, turning all black at maturity

Bloom: summer

Cycle/Origin: perennial, native

Habitat: sand ridges, dunes, wet woodland, swamps

Range: throughout

Stan's Notes: A diverse plant that grows on sandy ridges along the shores of the Great Lakes, and also in moist or wet woodland and swamps. The flowers are star-shaped, hence the common name. The flowers are found at the end (terminal) of the single zigzag stem. The flowers produce a cluster of large round berries, sometimes green and sometimes red, with nearly black bands. Berries turn nearly all black at maturity.

CLUSTER TYPE
Spike

FLOWER TYPE
Regular

LEAF TYPE
Simple

LEAF ATTACHMENT
Alternate

LEAF ATTACHMENT
Clasping

FRUIT
Berry

Garlic Mustard
Alliaria petiolata

Family: Mustard (Brassicaceae)

Height: 1–3' (30–90 cm)

Flower: a round cluster, 1–3" (2.5–7.5 cm) wide, of small white flowers; individual flowers, ¼" (.6 cm) wide, have 4 white petals

Leaf: heart-shaped lower leaves, 3–4" (7.5–10 cm) long, with sharp irregular teeth; smaller, triangular upper leaves, 1–2" (2.5–5 cm) long; all leaves smell strongly of garlic

Fruit: thin pod-like containers, up to 2" (5 cm) long

Bloom: spring, summer

Cycle/Origin: biennial, non-native

Habitat: wet, shade, deciduous woods

Range: throughout

Stan's Notes: A non-native plant of shady woodland borders and roadsides, Garlic Mustard was introduced from Europe. It was once commonly grown in gardens, where its flavorful leaves were cultivated for salads. Its leaves, stems and seed pods have a strong taste of garlic, and its tiny black seeds can be used as a pepper substitute. The four petals, arranged in a cross pattern, unmistakably identify Garlic Mustard as a member of the Mustard family. Seed pods split in half lengthwise to release many tiny black seeds.

CLUSTER TYPE
Round

FLOWER TYPE
Regular

LEAF TYPE
Simple

LEAF ATTACHMENT
Alternate

FRUIT
Pod

Miterwort
Mitella diphylla

Family: Saxifrage (Saxifragaceae)

Height: 8–18" (20–45 cm)

Flower: tiny white-to-cream flowers, ⅛" (.5 cm) wide, arranged in a spike, 1–3" (2.5–7.5 cm) tall, at the top of a single thin stem; each flower has 5 petal-like sepals and 5 unusual fringed petals

Leaf: basal leaves, 1–3" (2.5–7.5 cm) wide, on long stems, somewhat 3-lobed and toothed; usually only a single set of stem leaves (cauline), midway along the stem, opposite and lance-shaped with teeth

Bloom: spring, summer

Cycle/Origin: perennial, native

Habitat: moist woods

Range: throughout the L.P.

Stan's Notes: A sparsely leafed plant that often grows in large clusters. Only a single set of leaves located halfway along the single stem helps to identify this flower. The flower has very unusual fern-like petals. Also known as Bishop's Cap because the flowers are shaped like a small cap or a bishop's hat (called a miter). The species name *diphylla* refers to the single set of leaves midway along the stem.

CLUSTER TYPE
Spike

FLOWER TYPE
Regular

LEAF TYPE
Simple

LEAF ATTACHMENT
Opposite

LEAF ATTACHMENT
Basal

283

fruit

Red Baneberry
Actaea rubra

Family: Buttercup (Ranunculaceae)

Height: 8–24" (20–60 cm)

Flower: a dense, tight, round cluster, 1–3" (2.5–7.5 cm) wide, of tiny white flowers, each ¼" (.6 cm) wide

Leaf: each leaf has about 5–20 coarse-toothed, oval-shaped, 2" (5 cm) long, leaflets with pointed ends

Fruit: cluster of shiny red berries on a thin green stalk

Bloom: spring

Cycle/Origin: perennial, native

Habitat: wet, shade, deciduous woods

Range: throughout

Stan's Notes: A common perennial of moist deciduous woods, Red Baneberry's leaves and flowers sit in a compact ball at the top of the plant, giving it a bushy appearance. When its flowers open, the petals fall off, leaving just the white stamens. Flowers produce a cluster of shiny, deep red poisonous berries, each rising from its own thin stalk. While they probably won't cause death, its poisonous berries will cause illness if eaten. Nearly identical to White Baneberry (pg. 287), except for the berry color. Frequently has white berries.

CLUSTER TYPE
Round

LEAF TYPE
Twice Compound

LEAF ATTACHMENT
Alternate

FRUIT
Berry

285

fruit

White Baneberry
Actaea pachypoda

Family: Buttercup (Ranunculaceae)

Height: 1–2' (30–60 cm)

Flower: a dense, tight, slightly elongated cluster, 1–3" (2.5–7.5 cm), of tiny white flowers, each ¼" (.6 cm) wide

Leaf: each leaf has about 5–20 coarse-toothed, oval-shaped 2" (5 cm) long, leaflets with pointed ends

Fruit: cluster of shiny white berries, each with a single black spot, grow on a fleshy, reddened stalk

Bloom: spring

Cycle/Origin: perennial, native

Habitat: wet, shade, deciduous woods

Range: throughout

Stan's Notes: A common perennial of moist deciduous woods, White Baneberry's leaves and flowers sit in a compact ball at the top of the plant, giving it a bushy appearance. When its flowers open, the petals fall off, leaving just the white stamens. Flowers produce a cluster of shiny, white poisonous berries, each rising from a thicken reddish stalk. The common name Bane means "to cause death." While they probably won't cause death, its poisonous berries will cause illness if eaten. Nearly identical to Red Baneberry (pg. 285), except for the berry color. The white berries marked with a single black dot look like the eyes of an old china doll, providing its other common name, Doll's Eyes.

CLUSTER TYPE
Round

LEAF TYPE
Twice Compound

LEAF ATTACHMENT
Alternate

FRUIT
Berry

Northern Bedstraw
Galium boreale

Family: Madder (Rubiaceae)

Height: 10–36" (25–90 cm)

Flower: dense clusters, 1–3" (2.5–7.5 cm) wide, of tiny white flowers sit at the top of the stalk; each flower, ¼" (.6 cm) wide, has 4 petals that fuse together into a tube at the base

Leaf: a whorl of 4 very narrow, ¼" (.6 cm) wide, linear leaves, ¾–2" (2–5 cm) long, with a pointed end

Bloom: summer

Cycle/Origin: perennial, native

Habitat: dry, sun, prairies, fields, along roads

Range: throughout

Stan's Notes: Also called Snow Bedstraw because of its dense cluster of snow-white flowers, Northern Bedstraw often grows in large clumps and is an impressive sight when in bloom. A square-stemmed plant with a smooth stem and leaves, it is unlike many of the other bedstraws, which have sticky stems. One of at least 20 species of bedstraw in Michigan, a few of which have a pleasant fragrance when crushed. This plant was once used to stuff mattresses, hence the common name. A member of the same family as coffee, its roasted seeds brew a nice coffee substitute.

CLUSTER TYPE
Spike

FLOWER TYPE
Regular

LEAF TYPE
Simple

LEAF ATTACHMENT
Whorl

Common Shinleaf
Pyrola elliptica

Family: Heather (Ericaceae)

Height: 5–10" (12.5–25 cm)

Flower: open spike cluster, 1–3" (2.5–7.5 cm) long, of greenish white hanging bell-shaped flowers, ½" (1 cm) wide, that are very fragrant and on a single stem; bottom flowers open before the top flowers

Leaf: dark olive green, elliptical to round basal leaves, 1–3" (2.5–7.5 cm) long, with reddish leafstalk

Fruit: 5-chambered brown pod

Bloom: summer

Cycle/Origin: perennial, native

Habitat: dry deciduous woods, along streams and lakes

Range: throughout

Stan's Notes: One of several shinleaf species in Michigan, this is the most common of all. The evergreen leaves contain a chemical similar to aspirin. A plaster of mashed leaves and water used to reduce pain was called a shin plaster, hence the common name. About 30 species of Pyrola are found in the world.

CLUSTER TYPE
Spike

FLOWER TYPE
Bell

LEAF TYPE
Simple

LEAF ATTACHMENT
Basal

FRUIT
Pod

Long-fruited Thimbleweed
Anemone cylindrica

Family: Buttercup (Ranunculaceae)

Height: 2–3' (60–90 cm)

Flower: a long, thimble-shaped flower, 1¼–2" (3–5 cm) tall, with 5 white petal-like sepals, ¾" (2 cm) long; the center "thimble" is about three times as long as it is wide

Leaf: basal leaves are in a whorl of 3; each leaf, 3" (7.5 cm) long, is divided into 3–5 coarsely toothed lobes; leaves on the stem (cauline) look similar to basal leaves, only smaller

Bloom: summer

Cycle/Origin: perennial, native

Habitat: dry, sun, dry prairies

Range: throughout the L.P. and the southern U.P.

Stan's Notes: Also called Thimbleweed, one of five species of *Anemone* in Michigan. A single-stemmed hairy plant with two to ten sets of whorled leaves (each group of whorled leaves has two, three or five leaves). Several long flower stalks rise above the last set of leaves. The length of the flower center, or "thimble," differentiates the Long-fruited Thimbleweed from the Thimbleweed (pg. 245). Like some members of the Buttercup family, its flower lacks petals, and instead has large petal-like sepals. After pollination, the thimble-shaped seed heads turn cottony with many small seeds.

FLOWER TYPE
Regular

LEAF TYPE
Simple Lobed

LEAF ATTACHMENT
Basal

LEAF ATTACHMENT
Whorl

293

Wild Calla
Calla palustris

Family: Arum (Araceae)

Height: aquatic

Flower: a large white petal (spathe), 2" (5 cm) long, wraps around a 1" (2.5 cm) tall, club-like cluster (spadix) of tiny yellow flowers, ¼" (.6 cm) wide; the flower is held up to 6" (15 cm) above the water

Leaf: dark green, glossy, heart-shaped leaves, 6" (15 cm) long, on long stalks held above the water surface; leaves are deeply notched where the stalk attaches

Fruit: a tight cluster of bright red berries

Bloom: spring

Cycle/Origin: perennial, native

Habitat: wetlands, ponds, lakes, bogs

Range: throughout

Stan's Notes: Also called Water Arum or Wild Calla Lily, the Wild Calla is found in bogs and swamps. All parts of the plant contain oxalic acid, which causes an intense burning sensation if eaten. This plant is characterized by a very interesting two-part flower structure of a club-like spadix wrapped in a flat spathe. The flowers are actually very small and tightly packed at the base of the club-like spadix (very hard to see). It is closely related to Jack-in-the-pulpit (pg. 81).

CLUSTER TYPE	LEAF TYPE	LEAF ATTACHMENT	FRUIT
Spike	**Simple**	**Basal**	**Berry**

Hedge Bindweed
Calystegia sepium

Family: Morning Glory (Convolvulaceae)

Height: 3–10' (90–300 cm); climbing vine

Flower: white-to-pink, tube or funnel-shaped flowers, 2–3" (5–7.5 cm) long; 5 petals fuse together to form the tube flower

Leaf: arrowhead-shaped, toothless leaves, 2–4" (5–10 cm) long, alternate along a vine stem; the base of each leaf extends below its stalk attachment, giving the appearance of ears (basal lobes)

Fruit: papery pod-like container with 4 brown seeds

Bloom: summer, fall

Growth: perennial, native

Habitat: dry, sunny fields, along woodlands

Range: throughout

Stan's Notes: A climbing vine up to 10' (3 m) long, the Hedge Bindweed is often seen on old fences, open fields and climbing on shrubs. Its flowers are highly variable in color, ranging from pure white to pink. They open in the morning and close in the afternoon. Hedge Bindweed flowers will stay open all day if temperatures are cool, but will not open at all if too cold, and they usually only last one day. It is closely related to the Common Blue Garden Morning Glory and thirteen other species in North America; and is similar, but much larger than Field Bindweed (pg. 275).

FLOWER TYPE **Tube**   LEAF TYPE **Simple**   LEAF ATTACHMENT **Alternate**   FRUIT **Pod**

Boneset

Eupatorium perfoliatum

Family: Aster (Asteraceae)

Height: 2–4' (60–120 cm)

Flower: numerous, flat, white flowers, each ¼" (.6 cm) in diameter, in a large, flat-topped cluster, 2–3" (5–7.5 cm) wide; multiple tiny flowers give the appearance of a fuzzy cluster

Leaf: large, wrinkly, opposing leaves, 4–8" (10–20 cm) long, join at the base around the stem so that the stem appears to grow through the leaves (perfoliate)

Bloom: summer, fall

Cycle/Origin: perennial, native

Habitat: wet ditches, along roads, prairies, wet meadows

Range: throughout

Stan's Notes: A tall plant common at roadsides, the Boneset is easy to identify by its wrinkled leaves, which have large leaf bases that enclose the stem and make it appear as if the stem is actually growing through several large leaves. To some healers, this odd leaf growth meant that the plant was useful for setting bones, hence its common name. Boneset Tea, made from the plant's leaves, is said to treat colds and coughs and break fevers. Its stem and leaves are covered in fine whitish hairs. Closely related to Joe-pye Weed (pg. 133) and White Snakeroot (pg. 269), the Boneset is one of the few plants to bloom in late summer. A great nectar plant for Bronze Copper, Monarch, Crescent and Fritillary butterflies.

CLUSTER TYPE	FLOWER TYPE	LEAF TYPE	LEAF ATTACHMENT
Flat	**Composite**	**Simple**	**Perfoliate**

Turtlehead
Chelone glabra

Family: Plantain (Plantaginaceae)

Height: 1–3' (30–90 cm)

Flower: tight spike cluster, 2–3" (5–7.5 cm) tall, of many white (sometimes lavender) flowers, 1–1½" (2.5–4 cm) long; 2 petals fuse together to form a tube flower

Leaf: narrow, opposite, lance-shaped leaves, ½–1" (1–2.5 cm) wide and 3–6" (7.5–15 cm) long, with sharp teeth

Bloom: summer, fall

Cycle/Origin: perennial, native

Habitat: wet, sun, moist fields, along streams, wetlands

Range: throughout

Stan's Notes: Found growing along streams and wetlands, the Turtlehead often grows as a single stem topped with a cluster of large white flowers. The shape of the flower resembles the head of a turtle; hence the common name (the genus name, *Chelone*, is Greek for "tortoise"). Look for the narrow, sharp-toothed opposite leaves to help identify this wildflower. A host plant for the very rare Baltimore butterfly. Due to loss of habitat, the Turtlehead is not as common as it once was.

CLUSTER TYPE **Spike**   FLOWER TYPE **Tube**   LEAF TYPE **Simple**   LEAF ATTACHMENT **Opposite**

Labrador Tea
Rhododendron groenlandicum

Family: Heath (Ericaceae)

Height: 1–4' (30–120 cm), shrub

Flower: a collection of small white flowers, ⅓–½" (.8–1 cm) wide, form tight round clusters, 2–3" (5–7.5 cm) wide; individual flowers have 5 petals

Leaf: dark green, lance-shaped, evergreen leaves with an inward curled edge (margin) and dense, woolly, orange-brown hairs underneath; leaves are concentrated near the top of its woolly stem

Fruit: pod-like capsule with 5 openings to release seeds

Bloom: spring, summer

Cycle/Origin: perennial, native

Habitat: wet, shade, coniferous woods, peat bogs, cedar swamps

Range: northern half of the L.P. and the entire U.P.

Stan's Notes: Also known as Hudson's Bay Tea, Labrador Tea is a very common low shrub of the northern bogs. Its leaves contain an aromatic resin that makes a pleasant-tasting tea, and the unique woolly brown hair beneath its leaves makes it one of the easiest plants to identify. Labrador Tea's evergreen leaves remain on the plant year-round.

CLUSTER TYPE
Round

FLOWER TYPE
Regular

LEAF TYPE
Simple

LEAF ATTACHMENT
Alternate

FRUIT
Pod

Catnip
Nepeta cataria

Family: Mint (Lamiaceae)

Height: 1–3' (30–90 cm)

Flower: a tight spike cluster, 2–4" (5–10 cm) long, of white tube-like flowers, ½" (1 cm) long, made up of 2 large petals; each flower has purplish spots and can range in color from white to lavender

Leaf: opposite, coarsely toothed, arrowhead-shaped leaves, 1–3" (2.5–7.5 cm) long, covered with soft, white, downy hairs; very aromatic when crushed

Bloom: summer, fall

Cycle/Origin: perennial, non-native

Habitat: dry, sun or shade, fields, gardens, along roads, near buildings

Range: throughout

Stan's Notes: A non-native plant thought to come from Asia but probably introduced from Europe as a garden herb, Catnip has been used as a medicinal tea. It contains a terpene, nepetalactone, which works to repel insects. This chemical also attracts cats, from lions to cougars to house cats. Its skunk-like odor and soft downy white hairs help identify this plant, while its square stem and opposite leaves distinguish it as a member of the Mint family.

CLUSTER TYPE
Spike

FLOWER TYPE
Tube

LEAF TYPE
Simple

LEAF ATTACHMENT
Opposite

Common Yarrow
Achillea millefolium

Family: Aster (Asteraceae)

Height: 1–3' (30–90 cm)

Flower: tight, flat-topped, white (sometimes pink) flower clusters, 2–4" (5–10 cm) wide, made up of tiny flower heads, ¼" (.6 cm) wide, each with 4–6 (usually 5) petals

Leaf: narrow, finely divided, fern-like, feathery leaves about 6" (15 cm) long, have a strong aroma and become progressively smaller toward the top; those at the plant's base are stalked, while the upper leaves are not

Bloom: summer, fall

Cycle/Origin: perennial, native

Habitat: dry, sun, deciduous woods, fields, prairies

Range: throughout

Stan's Notes: A common wildflower of open fields and along roads, this is one of three species of *Achillea* found in Michigan. A native of Eurasia as well as North America, it is uncertain which of our plants were introduced or are native. Often confused with a type of fern because of its leaves, this wildflower grows in large clusters due to a horizontal underground stem (rhizome). The genus name, *Achillea*, comes from the legend that Achilles used the plant to treat bleeding wounds during the Trojan War. The species name, *millefolium*, means "thousand leaves," and refers to each leaf's many divisions, making one leaf look like many. Many cultures have used it as a medicinal herb.

CLUSTER TYPE
Flat

FLOWER TYPE
Composite

LEAF TYPE
Simple Lobed

LEAF ATTACHMENT
Alternate

Large-flowered Trillium
Trillium grandiflorum

Family: Bunchflower (Melanthiaceae)

Height: 8–18" (20–45 cm)

Flower: a single white flower, 2–4" (5–10 cm) wide, grows from a single stalk; 3 white, triangle-shaped, wavy-edged petals are set against 3 pointed, green, petal-like sepals, which look like green petals

Leaf: 3 large, pointed, toothless broad leaves, 3–6" (7.5–15 cm) long, with veins that extend to the leaf's edge

Fruit: a single red berry, 1" (2.5 cm) wide

Bloom: spring

Cycle/Origin: perennial, native

Habitat: rich moist woodlands, deciduous woods

Range: throughout

Stan's Notes: Also called White-flowered Trillium, the Large-flowered Trillium is one of nine species of trillium found in Michigan. This species has the largest flower, hence its common and scientific names. It is a protected flower species that should never be picked or dug up (it can be purchased from garden centers, but make sure plants are cultivated from non-wild stock). The Large-flowered Trillium blooms early in spring, occurring alone or in groups, and its white flowers turn pink with age. Seeds are dispersed by ants that carry the seeds back to their underground homes, but don't eat them.

FLOWER TYPE
Regular

LEAF TYPE
Simple

LEAF ATTACHMENT
Whorl

FRUIT
Berry

Virgin's Bower
Clematis virginiana

Family: Buttercup (Ranunculaceae)

Height: 6–10' (1.8–3 m) climbing vine

Flower: delicate round clusters, 2–4" (5–10 cm) wide, of white flowers, 1" (2.5 cm) wide, with 4 or 5 petal-like sepals with a center of many thin, greenish yellow, hair-like flower parts (stamens and anthers)

Leaf: a 3-part leaf, with each leaflet sharply toothed or lobed, 2" (5 cm) long

Fruit: a group of single seeds, each attached to a single curvy, white, hair-like projection

Bloom: summer

Cycle/Origin: perennial, native

Habitat: shade, along edges of woods

Range: throughout the U.P.

Stan's Notes: Also called Old Man's Beard, this is one of only two *Clematis* species in Michigan. Purple Virgin's Bower (not shown) grows in the U.P. only and features a large blue flower similar to the garden clematis, its close relative. This square-stemmed perennial vine is usually seen growing over fences or shrubs or along riverbanks. Late in summer and fall, the hairy plumes of its pollinated female flowers look like a frosted vine. Seed head has curvy, white hair-like projections, giving the plant the appearance of an old man's beard. This plant can be grown from seed, but it should never be dug from the wild.

CLUSTER TYPE
Round

FLOWER TYPE
Regular

LEAF TYPE
Compound

LEAF ATTACHMENT
Opposite

leaf

Water Hemlock

Cicuta maculata

Family: Carrot (Apiaceae)

Height: 3–6' (90–180 cm)

Flower: delicate flat-topped clusters, 2–4" (5–10 cm) wide, of tiny white flowers, ⅛" (.5 cm) wide

Leaf: lower leaves are larger and sometimes twice compound; upper leaves are compound with individual leaflets, 1" (2.5 cm) long, sharply pointed and toothed, with veins that end at the notches between the teeth

Bloom: summer, fall

Cycle/Origin: perennial, native

Habitat: wet, sun, ditches, along roads, wet meadows

Range: throughout the L.P.

Stan's Notes: A common plant of wet pastures and along roads and ditches, Water Hemlock is by far the most poisonous plant in Michigan. A member of the Carrot family, its long taproot smells and tastes like carrot, but just a small amount will lead to convulsions and death. To help correctly identify this dangerous plant, look for the unique network of veins along its toothed leaves. The veins end at the notches between the teeth (as opposed to more common veining of other plants, which run to the tip of the tooth). This plant is closely related to the hemlock that poisoned Socrates.

CLUSTER TYPE	FLOWER TYPE	LEAF TYPE	LEAF ATTACHMENT	LEAF ATTACHMENT
Flat	**Regular**	**Compound**	**Alternate**	**Clasping**

Tall Meadow Rue
Thalictrum dasycarpum

Family: Buttercup (Ranunculaceae)

Height: 2–8' (60–240 cm)

Flower: round plumy clusters, 3–4" (7.5–10 cm) wide, of dangling whitish green flowers; individual flowers, ⅓" (.8 cm) wide, lack petals and instead have many showy, yellowish, thread-like flower parts (stamens) hanging down

Leaf: bluish green leaves made of up to 25 leaflets; each leaflet, 1" (2.5 cm) long, has 3 tooth-like lobes

Bloom: summer

Cycle/Origin: perennial, native

Habitat: wet, shade, wetlands, along streams

Range: throughout

Stan's Notes: Sometimes a very difficult species to identify correctly, Tall Meadow Rue is a very tall plant with characteristic dark red-to-purple stems and bluish green leaves. Found in wetlands and along streams, it is one of at least four species of *Thalictrum* in Michigan. Its petals fall off shortly after the flower opens, leaving only the male and female flower parts (stamen and pistils). Its flowers are wind pollinated, but are also visited by bees, butterflies and other insects. Very similar to the shorter Early Meadow Rue (pg. 79).

CLUSTER TYPE
Round

FLOWER TYPE
Bell

LEAF TYPE
Twice Compound

LEAF ATTACHMENT
Alternate

flower

Queen Anne's Lace
Daucus carota

Family: Carrot (Apiaceae)

Height: 1–3' (30–90 cm)

Flower: a flat cluster, 3–5" (7.5–12.5 cm) wide, of tiny white flowers, each ¼" (.6 cm) wide; a single purple-to-black floret sits near the cluster's center, with 3 thin, forked, green bracts beneath the cluster

Leaf: fern-like, with many divisions, up to 8" (20 cm) long

Bloom: summer, fall

Cycle/Origin: biennial, non-native

Habitat: dry, sun, fields, along roads, disturbed soils

Range: throughout

Stan's Notes: Queen Anne's Lace, also called Wild Carrot, is tall with stems covered by tiny hairs. Once a European garden plant, it has escaped to the wild and is considered a weed because of its aggressive growth. Flower clusters dry and curl, forming the bird's nest shape often used in dried flower arrangements. Its long taproot can be dug up, roasted and ground as a coffee substitute. During its first year, the roots are soft enough to eat. It is thought to be the ancestor of the common garden carrot. Take caution: Queen Anne's Lace is sometimes confused with the deadly Water Hemlock (pg. 313). Look closely for Queen Anne's Lace's central purple floret. A host plant for Black Swallowtail butterfly caterpillars.

CLUSTER TYPE
Flat

FLOWER TYPE
Regular

LEAF TYPE
Twice Compound

LEAF ATTACHMENT
Alternate

fruit

False Solomon's Seal

Maianthemum racemosum

Family: Asparagus (Asparagaceae)

Height: 1–3' (30–90 cm)

Flower: tiny, star-shaped, white flowers, ⅛" (.3 cm) wide, grow at the end of a single, long, arching stem to form a cluster, 3–5" (7.5–12.5 cm) long; each flower is made up of 3 petals and 3 petal-like sepals, giving the appearance of 6 petals

Leaf: oval, stalkless leaves, 3–6" (7.5–15 cm) long, hairy underneath with heavy parallel veining

Fruit: a cluster of waxy red berries

Bloom: spring, summer

Cycle/Origin: perennial, native

Habitat: deciduous woods

Range: throughout

Stan's Notes: A spike flower cluster at the end of the stem of the False Solomon's Seal distinguishes it from Smooth Solomon's Seal (pg. 71), whose flowers hang beneath the stem. Very similar to Star-flowered Solomon's Seal (pg. 279), which has larger flowers. This woodland perennial grows on the forest floor from an elongated horizontal rootstock. Its waxy red berries are not edible. A round scar on the rhizome (left after the stem has broken off) resembles the seal of King Solomon, hence "Solomon's Seal" in the common name.

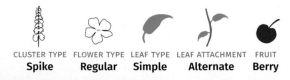

CLUSTER TYPE	FLOWER TYPE	LEAF TYPE	LEAF ATTACHMENT	FRUIT
Spike	**Regular**	**Simple**	**Alternate**	**Berry**

319

White Water Lily
Nymphaea odorata

Family: Water Lily (Nymphaeaceae)

Height: aquatic

Flower: floating white flowers, 3–6" (7.5–15 cm) wide, made up of many pointed petals surrounding a yellow center

Leaf: round or heart-shaped, deeply notched, toothless, shiny, green, floating leaves, 5–12" (12.5–30 cm) wide

Bloom: summer, fall

Cycle/Origin: perennial, native

Habitat: small lakes, channels, bays

Range: throughout

Stan's Notes: Also called Fragrant Water Lily. The White Water Lily's leaves float directly on the water's surface. This common pond lily requires quiet water because it is rooted to the lake or pond bottom. Its roots produce large tubers that are often eaten by muskrats. Its stems and leaves have air channels that trap air to keep the plant afloat. Flowers open on sunny days and close at night and on cloudy days. A second species of water lily found in Michigan is the Small White Water Lily (*N. leibergii*); it occurs only in the far north and has white flowers half as large as the White Water Lily.

FLOWER TYPE
Regular

LEAF TYPE
Simple

LEAF ATTACHMENT
Basal

fruit

Wild Cucumber

Echinocystis lobata

Family: Gourd (Cucurbitaceae)

Height: 2–10' (60–300 cm); climbing vine

Flower: male flowers are showy, large, round clusters, 4–8" (10–20 cm) long; individual flowers, 6 thin petals, ½" (1 cm) wide, on erect stalks rising from a leaf joint; single female flower found at base of male flower stalk

Leaf: large maple-like leaves, each with 5 sharply divided lobes culminating in a point resembling a 5-pointed star

Fruit: single large, green pod-like container that turns to brown; 2" (5 cm) long, covered in rubbery spines that dries to a papery, skeleton-like, brown shell containing 4 seeds, each in its own chamber

Bloom: summer, fall

Cycle/Origin: annual, native

Habitat: wet, shade, deciduous woods

Range: throughout

Stan's Notes: Sometimes called Balsam Apple, this plant looks similar to the Bur Cucumber (pg. 265), but grows in wetter areas. It has long, curly forked tendrils and a square stem, and its leaves, flowers stalks and tendrils all arise from the same point on the vine. Its large fruit smells and tastes like cucumber, but will cause upset stomach and diarrhea. In flower it may appear as a mass of white flowers climbing over a shrub. The fruit dries to a papery, skeleton-like appearance, giving it the nickname, "Lace Pants."

CLUSTER TYPE
Round

FLOWER TYPE
Regular

LEAF TYPE
Simple Lobed

LEAF ATTACHMENT
Alternate

FRUIT
Pod

Cow Parsnip

Heracleum sphondylium ssp. *montanum*

Family: Carrot (Apiaceae)

Height: 4–9' (1.2–2.7 m)

Flower: a very large flat cluster, 4–8" (10–20 cm) wide, of white (sometimes purplish) flowers; individual flowers, ½" (1 cm) wide, have notched petals and are often larger toward the outer edges of the cluster

Leaf: an extremely large leaf, up to 12" (30 cm) wide, divided into 3 maple-like segments, 3–6" (7.5–15 cm) long; each is coarsely toothed and does not connect to one another; leafstalk is grossly swollen or inflated near the ridged and hollow main stem

Bloom: spring, summer

Cycle/Origin: perennial, native

Habitat: sun, moist areas along roads, lakes and streams

Range: throughout

Stan's Notes: A very tall, single-stemmed plant with large leaves and flat clusters of white flowers, the Cow Parsnip is often confused with the much smaller poisonous Water Hemlock (pg. 313). The Cow Parsnip's stem is grooved and hollow and, when the plant is bruised or cut, it emits a very rank odor. Look for the large inflated leafstalk (swelling) to help identify this plant, commonly found growing in wet or moist soil.

CLUSTER TYPE
Flat

FLOWER TYPE
Regular

LEAF TYPE
Simple Lobed

LEAF ATTACHMENT
Alternate

Flat-topped Aster
Doellingeria umbellata

Family: Aster (Asteraceae)

Height: 1–6' (30–180 cm)

Flower: a flat cluster, 6–10" (15–25 cm) wide, of creamy white flower heads, ½–¾" (1–2 cm) wide; each flower head has 10–15 petals (ray flowers) with a yellow center (disk flowers)

Leaf: pointed, toothless, lance-shaped leaves, 3–6" (7.5–15 cm) long, alternate along the main stem

Bloom: summer, fall

Cycle/Origin: perennial, native

Habitat: wet, sun, edges of woods, swamps, prairies

Range: throughout

Stan's Notes: One of the first asters to bloom each summer, Flat-topped Aster grows a white flat cluster of flowers that attracts many insects. A single-stemmed plant with alternate leaves crowded along the stem, it grows in moist fields and along the edges of woods. Its center of yellow disk flowers turns purple with age. Its large flat cluster of flower heads makes it one of the easiest asters to identify. Like other asters, Flat-topped Aster has composite flowers. Each flower is composed of white ray flowers and yellow disk flowers. Once the ray flowers are shed, the seed head and flattened bracts look like tiny stars. A host plant for Pearl Crescent and Silvery Checkerspot butterfly caterpillars.

CLUSTER TYPE	FLOWER TYPE	LEAF TYPE	LEAF ATTACHMENT
Flat	**Composite**	**Simple**	**Alternate**

White Sweet Clover
Melilotus albus

Family: Pea or Bean (Fabaceae)

Height: 3–6' (90–180 cm)

Flower: long spike clusters, 8" (20 cm) tall, of white pea-like flowers, ¼" (.6 cm) long; each grows on a short stalk

Leaf: each leaf divides into 3 narrow, toothed, lance-shaped leaflets, ½–1" (1–2.5 cm) long

Fruit: egg-shaped pod

Bloom: spring, summer, fall

Cycle/Origin: annual or biennial, non-native

Habitat: wet or dry, sun, along roads, open fields

Range: throughout

Stan's Notes: A non-native plant introduced from Europe via Eurasia, White Sweet Clover was once grown as a hay crop, but has escaped and now grows throughout Michigan along roads and fields. This plant, along with Yellow Sweet Clover, is a major source of nectar for the Honeybee to make honey. Seeds can lie dormant in soil for decades until soil is disturbed and seeds come to within 2" (5 cm) of the surface. The amount of light in the 2" (5 cm) of soil is enough to trigger germination. This very fragrant plant smells like vanilla when its leaves or flowers are crushed. The genus name, *Melilotus*, is Greek for "honey," referring to its use as a nectar source for bees. Nearly identical to the Yellow Sweet Clover (pg. 415), except for the flower color.

CLUSTER TYPE
Spike

FLOWER TYPE
Irregular

LEAF TYPE
Compound

LEAF ATTACHMENT
Alternate

FRUIT
Pod

Culver's Root

Veronicastrum virginicum

Family: Plantain (Plantaginaceae)

Height: 3–5' (90–150 cm)

Flower: many white tube-shaped flowers, ¼" (.6 cm) long, form a tapering spike cluster that grows up to 10–12" (25–30 cm) long; individual flower tubes are made up of 4 fused petals

Leaf: slender, finely toothed, lance-shaped leaves, 2–6" (5–15 cm) long, whorl around each stem in groups of 3–7

Bloom: summer

Cycle/Origin: perennial, native

Habitat: prairies, meadows, fields, along railroad tracks

Range: southern half of the L.P.

Stan's Notes: A tall showy plant of native prairies, Culver's Root can still be found along railroad beds and roads. Used by American pioneers as a medicinal plant because its roots contain several toxic chemicals, and its sap contains a strong emetic and laxative. This member of the Broomrape family is closely related to several cultivated garden plants. Some plants have only one spike, while others have three to five. Bees are especially attracted to its flowers.

CLUSTER TYPE	FLOWER TYPE	LEAF TYPE	LEAF ATTACHMENT
Spike	**Tube**	**Simple**	**Whorl**

Black Medick
Medicago lupulina

Family: Pea or Bean (Fabaceae)

Height: 1–2" (2.5–5 cm)

Flower: many tiny, yellow flowers, ⅛" (.3 cm) long, form a small round cluster, ¼" (.6 cm) long; each cluster consists of 20–25 individual flowers and sits at the end of a thin stalk

Leaf: typical clover-type leaves, ¼–½" (.6–1 cm) long, made up of 3 round leaflets, each with fine teeth along the edge, and a single, tiny, sharp point at the end

Fruit: tiny, twisted black seed pod, ⅛–¼" (.3–.6 cm) long

Bloom: spring, summer

Cycle/Origin: annual, non-native

Habitat: dry, sun, lawns, along roads

Range: throughout

Stan's Notes: A very low-growing and small prostrate plant most often seen growing in lawns or along roads, Black Medick is a native of Eurasia that has spread throughout Michigan. Its stems are covered with short, soft, whitish hairs, giving them a fuzzy appearance. It is considered a weed because it grows in lawns. Very common but so small it is often overlooked. The Medick seeds are a very important food for migrant sparrows in the fall.

CLUSTER TYPE	LEAF TYPE	LEAF ATTACHMENT	FRUIT
Round	**Compound**	**Alternate**	**Pod**

Leafy Spurge
Euphorbia esula

Family: Spurge (Euphorbiaceae)

Height: 1–2' (30–60 cm)

Flower: flat cluster, 2–3" (5–7.5 cm) wide, of 15–25 yellow green flowers; individual flower is actually 2 large colored bracts that surround an extremely small green flower, ⅛" (.3 cm) wide

Leaf: narrow lance-shaped leaves, 1–3" (2.5–7.5 cm) long, lacking a leaf stem; milky sap oozes when broken

Bloom: spring, summer

Cycle/Origin: perennial, non-native

Habitat: dry, sun, fields, along roads, in disturbed soils

Range: throughout

Stan's Notes: A very aggressive European import officially considered a noxious weed in Michigan. A colored, petal-like bract, not actual petals, characterizes this and other members of the Spurge family (the Christmas Poinsettia is a good example of petal-like red bracts, which are not true flowers). Its stems and leaves contain a white, very sticky, milky sap, and it spreads along a horizontal, underground root system (rhizome). If its rootstock is cut up in an attempt to eradicate it, each root section will grow into a new plant. Because of this, special beetles are now being released to eat it in an attempt to control its aggressive growth. The common name, "Spurge," comes from the Latin *expurgare* (to purge), describing the laxative properties of this poisonous plant.

CLUSTER TYPE   LEAF TYPE   LEAF ATTACHMENT
Flat   **Simple**   **Alternate**

Birds-foot Trefoil
Lotus corniculatus

Family: Pea or Bean (Fabaceae)

Height: 6–24" (15–60 cm)

Flower: showy, yellow, pea-like flowers, ½" (1 cm) long, clustered in a large mass of flowers

Leaf: a 5-part compound leaf made up of 3-part upper clover-like leaflets and 2 lower leaflets at the stalk base

Fruit: slender, 3–5, parted, pea-like pods, about 1" (2.5 cm) long

Bloom: spring, summer, fall

Cycle/Origin: perennial, non-native

Habitat: dry, sunny, old fields, especially along roads

Range: throughout

Stan's Notes: A non-native plant introduced from Europe as a cultivated forage crop, the Birds-foot Trefoil was widely planted for erosion control along newly constructed roads. It can be very aggressive and take over disturbed soils very quickly. Its flowers start out a bright lemon yellow but turn reddish orange with age. Its common name refers in part to its seed pods, which together look like a bird's foot, and its leaves, which mistakenly appear to grow in threes, hence "tre" foil. There are about 140 species worldwide in its genus, with around 40 found in the U.S., mostly in western states. A nectar source for European Skipper and Sulphur butterflies.

FLOWER TYPE
Irregular

LEAF TYPE
Compound

LEAF ATTACHMENT
Alternate

FRUIT
Pod

Yellow Wood Sorrel
Oxalis stricta

Family: Wood Sorrel (Oxalidaceae)

Height: 6–15" (15–37.5 cm)

Flower: 1 to many, bright yellow flowers, ½" (1 cm) wide, made up of 5 petals

Leaf: each leaf is divided into 3 heart-shaped leaflets, resembling a compound clover leaf

Fruit: narrow pod-like capsule, ½" (1 cm) long, standing upright on a thin stalk

Bloom: spring, summer, fall

Cycle/Origin: annual, native

Habitat: dry, sun, disturbed soils, gardens, along roads

Range: throughout

Stan's Notes: Also called Oxalis, Yellow Wood Sorrel is a weak-stemmed plant that often grows unwanted in gardens. The leaves, stems and seed pods of this edible plant have a sour taste (the genus name, *Oxalis*, is Greek for "sour," and children often call it Sour Grass). Caution should be taken, however, as the plant contains oxalic acid which can cause upset stomach. Because it contains a high concentration of Vitamin C, phosphorus and potassium, Yellow Wood Sorrel has been used as a folk medicine to treat many ailments. It produces many seeds, which become food for juncos and sparrows.

FLOWER TYPE
Regular

LEAF TYPE
Compound

LEAF ATTACHMENT
Alternate

FRUIT
Pod

339

Tufted Loosestrife
Lysimachia thyrsiflora

Family: Primrose (Primulaceae)

Height: 1–3' (30–90 cm)

Flower: 3–5 compact dense clusters, ½–1" (1–2.5 cm) long, of yellow tiny flowers, ¼" (.6 cm) long, on tall flower stalks arising from the leaf axis near the middle of the plant, not at the top as one might expect

Leaf: pairs of narrow lance-shaped leaves, 2–6" (5–15 cm) long, lacking teeth; slightly hairy along the midrib beneath each leaf; leaves near the top of plant are often deformed by disease

Bloom: summer

Cycle/Origin: perennial, native

Habitat: wetlands, swamps, wet meadows, bogs

Range: throughout

Stan's Notes: A native loosestrife that produces dense tufts of yellow flowers, hence the common name. Flowers occur midway up the single stem. This plant can often be hidden by other taller wetland plants. The underside of each leaf can be hairy along the midrib. Found growing in groups in nearly any wet place. At least seven species of loosestrife in North America, most preferring moist or wet soils.

CLUSTER TYPE
Round

LEAF TYPE
Simple

LEAF ATTACHMENT
Opposite

Downy Yellow Violet

Viola pubescens

Family: Violet (Violaceae)

Height: 8–16" (20–40 cm)

Flower: several yellow flowers per plant; individual flower, ¾" (2 cm) wide, made up of 5 petals with several dark purple veins; each flower grows on its own stalk

Leaf: hairy heart-shaped leaves with round or scalloped teeth, alternately attached to the main stem

Bloom: spring, summer

Cycle/Origin: perennial, native

Habitat: wet, cool, shade, deciduous woods

Range: throughout

Stan's Notes: One of the few "stalked" violets, the Downy Yellow Violet's flowers arise on stalks that originate from a leaf attachment (axis) rather than the more typical basal flower stalk. Its stalks (and to a lesser degree, its leaves) are covered with "down" hairs, hence the common name. This hairiness also helps to differentiate it from the many other yellow violets. The purple veins are guidelines or "come-ons" for pollinating insects to get to the pollen and nectar. The seed capsule acts like a shotgun. As the capsule dries, it compresses, bursts and shoots the seeds in all directions.

FLOWER TYPE
Irregular

LEAF TYPE
Simple

LEAF ATTACHMENT
Alternate

Ground Cherry
Physalis heterophylla

Family: Nightshade (Solanaceae)

Height: 6½–12" (16–30 cm)

Flower: pale yellow, bell-shaped flowers, ¾" (1.9 cm) long, with dark purple centers, arise from the upper stem's leafstalk junctions (axis) and hang straight down; 5 petals fuse together to form the bell-shaped flowers

Leaf: lance-shaped leaves, up to 2½" (6.3 cm) long, with infrequent teeth, sit on a short leafstalk

Fruit: inflated, green, papery husk harbors a green berry that turns orange to reddish orange when mature

Bloom: spring, summer

Cycle/Origin: perennial, native

Habitat: dry, sun, prairies, old fields

Range: throughout the L.P.

Stan's Notes: The Ground Cherry's unique inflated fruit looks like the fruit of the Chinese Lantern (*P. alkekengi*) (not shown), a garden plant with white flowers and red fruit. Its leaves resemble those of its close relative, the tomato. Once used as a medicinal plant, the Ground Cherry's ripe fruit is edible, but its unripe green fruit is toxic, and grazing animals that eat it have been poisoned. Its leaf shape gives it its other common name, the Lance-leaved Ground Cherry. A host plant for the caterpillars of Sphinx Moths (also known as Hummingbird Moths).

FLOWER TYPE	LEAF TYPE	LEAF ATTACHMENT	FRUIT
Bell	**Simple**	**Alternate**	**Berry**

Fringed Loosestrife

Lysimachia ciliata

Family: Primrose (Primulaceae)

Height: 1–4' (30–120 cm)

Flower: nodding yellow flowers, ¾–1" (2–2.25 cm) wide, with 5 fringed petals; flowers rise from the axis of the leaves

Leaf: pairs of oval to lance-shaped opposite leaves, 2–6" (5–15 cm) long, lacking teeth, with fringed or hairy leafstalks

Bloom: summer

Cycle/Origin: perennial, native

Habitat: wetlands, wet woodland, wet meadows

Range: throughout

Stan's Notes: A native loosestrife that produces attractive five-petal flowers with fringed petals, hence the common name. The leafstalks also contribute to the common name, since they are fringed or hairy. Tends to like wetter soils along streams and ponds. There are around 160 species of loosestrife worldwide, with approximately 20 found in North America, most of which prefer moist or wet soils.

FLOWER TYPE
Regular

LEAF TYPE
Simple

LEAF ATTACHMENT
Opposite

Canada Hawkweed
Hieracium umbellatum

Family: Aster (Asteraceae)

Height: 1–3' (30–90 cm)

Flower: 4–10 bright yellow, dandelion-like flowers, ¾–1" (2–2.5 cm) wide, grow on a single stalk and only open a few at a time; a composite flower, it is made up of 20–30 individual ray flowers, lacking the center disk flowers

Leaf: coarse-toothed, linear basal leaves, 2–5" (5–12.5 cm) long; stem leaves 1" (2.5 cm) long (cauline) stalkless with sharp teeth

Bloom: summer

Cycle/Origin: perennial, non-native

Habitat: dry, sun, fields, along roads, sandy soils, pastures

Range: throughout

Stan's Notes: This is one of fifteen species of Hawkweed that grow in Michigan, and it is often hard to correctly identify each species. This single-stemmed plant holds up to ten flowers that close at night and on cloudy days. After pollination, its flower heads produce a dandelion-like silk to carry away the seeds, further spreading the plant. It mainly reproduces by spreading leafy runners (stolon) across the ground. The name "Hawkweed" came from the mistaken belief that hawks ate the flowers to improve their vision. Similar to Orange Hawkweed (pg. 85).

FLOWER TYPE
Composite

LEAF TYPE
Simple

LEAF ATTACHMENT
Alternate

LEAF ATTACHMENT
Basal

Wild Oats

Uvularia sessilifolia

Family: Colchicum (Colchicaceae)

Height: 6–12" (15–30 cm)

Flower: usually 1, but sometimes 2, pale yellow, drooping, bell flowers, 1" (2.5 cm) long; individual flower has 6 petals, (actually 3 petals and 3 petal-like sepals) at the end of a forked stem

Leaf: lance-shaped leaves, 1–3" (2.5–7.5 cm) long, light green with a whitish underside; stalkless

Bloom: spring

Cycle/Origin: perennial, native

Habitat: deciduous woods

Range: southeastern half of the L.P.

Stan's Notes: A common woodland perennial, similar to the Large-flowered Bellwort (pg. 369), Wild Oats is sometimes called Sessile-leaved Bellwort. "Sessile" refers to the fact that the leaves lack leafstalks. "Bell" refers to the shape of the flower and "wort" means "plant." Usually a single-stemmed plant that forks into two stalks with a flower at the end of only one stalk. Once thought to have medicinal properties to treat throat disorders because the droopy flowers resemble the uvula, the soft lobe hanging in the back of your throat (genus name, *Uvularia*).

FLOWER TYPE
Bell

LEAF TYPE
Simple

LEAF ATTACHMENT
Alternate

Common St. Johnswort

Hypericum perforatum

Family: St. Johnswort (Hypericaceae)

Height: 1–3' (30–90 cm)

Flower: an open cluster of up to 20 bright yellow flowers, 1" (2.5 cm) wide, each with 5 petals with black dots on each petal edge (margin); many long and thin protruding flower parts (stamens)

Leaf: narrow, stalkless lance-shaped leaves, 1–2" (2.5–5 cm) long, with many translucent dots

Bloom: summer, fall

Cycle/Origin: perennial, non-native

Habitat: dry, sun, fields, roadsides, disturbed soils

Range: throughout

Stan's Notes: A non-native plant of roadsides and fields, Common St. Johnswort is a highly branched plant. The dots on its leaves, best seen if a leaf is held up to light, are actually oil-filled glands. Introduced from Europe, its common name comes from the fact that the flower blooms on or near June 24, St. John's Day ("wort" means "plant"). It is often used in folk medicine to treat eye problems and respiratory illnesses, and many of these medicinal uses have been recently revived. Dried leaves were also a talisman against witches and thunder, and a tea made of the leaves was used to relieve depression.

FLOWER TYPE | LEAF TYPE | LEAF ATTACHMENT
Regular | **Simple** | **Opposite**

Gumweed

Grindelia squarrosa

Family: Aster (Asteraceae)

Height: 6–36" (15–90 cm)

Flower: 3–20 yellow flower heads, 1" (2.5 cm) wide, with 20 or more short petals (ray flowers) that surround a central yellow disk (disk flowers); green, outward-curling bracts surround each flower head and exude a sticky gum-like resin

Leaf: simple oval leaves, 1–2½" (2.5–6 cm) long, often with wavy or curled edges and coarse teeth, usually lacking a leafstalk

Bloom: summer, fall

Cycle/Origin: perennial, non-native

Habitat: dry, sun, fields, along roads, disturbed soils

Range: throughout

Stan's Notes: Also called Gum Plant, Sticky Heads or Tarweed, its many common names refer to the sticky resin secreted from the bracts that surround each flower head. Gumweed resin will stain your hands and has been used by many cultures as a medicine for everything from asthma to healing wounds. A plant of the American West that has now expanded its range eastward, Gumweed is one of the first plants to grow after construction or in heavily grazed fields, and is commonly seen along roads and railroads. Its flower heads are commonly used in arrangements of dried flowers.

FLOWER TYPE **Composite**   LEAF TYPE **Simple**   LEAF ATTACHMENT **Alternate**

Jewelweed
Impatiens pallida

Family: Touch-me-not (Balsaminaceae)

Height: 3–5' (90–150 cm)

Flower: yellow tube flowers, 1" (2.5 cm) long, with a few dark reddish brown spots deep within their throats; each flower has a large open mouth that leads to a long, thin, downward-curved spur, containing nectar

Leaf: sharply toothed oval leaves, 1–4" (2.5–10 cm) long, on a short leafstalk

Fruit: thin, banana-shaped, green pod-like container

Bloom: summer

Cycle/Origin: annual, native

Habitat: wet, shade, wetlands, along streams

Range: southern half of the L.P.

Stan's Notes: Also called Pale Touch-me-not, the Jewelweed is so named because water droplets on its leaves shine like tiny jewels. This tall annual plant of wet areas has nearly translucent stems that contain a slippery juice that can be used to soothe the sting from nettles or Poison Ivy. Its long, thin ripe seed pods explode when touched, throwing seeds in all directions. This action provides its alternative common name, Touch-me-not. A similar species, Spotted Touch-me-not (pg. 87), has orange flowers with many dark red spots. A great flower to attract hummingbirds.

FLOWER TYPE
Tube

LEAF TYPE
Simple

LEAF ATTACHMENT
Alternate

FRUIT
Pod

Swamp Buttercup
Ranunculus hispidus

Family: Buttercup (Ranunculaceae)

Height: 1–3' (30–90 cm)

Flower: showy yellow flowers, 1" (2.5 cm) wide, grow on erect stalks above the leaves; individual flowers have 5 round, bright yellow petals

Leaf: distinct 3-lobed leaves, 3–4" (7.5–10 cm) wide, grow on long stalks; each lobe is again divided into 3 lobes with sharp teeth

Fruit: cluster of green, beaked, seed pods; each pod contains a winged seed

Bloom: spring, summer

Cycle/Origin: perennial, native

Habitat: wet, shade, deciduous woods, meadows, along streams, neglected gardens

Range: throughout

Stan's Notes: A large robust plant with long, hollow, arching stems, Swamp Buttercup often spreads by rooting where its stems touch the ground, eventually forming large clusters. The plant is very deeply rooted and difficult to remove if grown in a garden. Swamp Buttercup's common name comes from its habit of growing in wet soils and the "cup" shape of its "buttery" yellow flowers. Its flowers produce much pollen but little nectar, so it attracts pollen-eating beetles, flies and bees.

FLOWER TYPE
Regular

LEAF TYPE
Simple Lobed

LEAF ATTACHMENT
Alternate

FRUIT
Pod

Yellow Trout Lily
Erythronium americanum

Family: Lily (Liliaceae)

Height: 5–10" (12.5–25 cm)

Flower: each stalk produces a single hanging yellow flower, 1" (2.5 cm) wide; each flower has 6 backward-curving petals (actually 3 petals and 3 petal-like sepals)

Leaf: a pair of elliptical, pointed basal leaves, up to 8" (20 cm) long, with brownish purple spots and streaks, giving it a mottled look

Fruit: egg-shaped, green pod-like capsule

Bloom: spring

Cycle/Origin: perennial, native

Habitat: dry, deciduous woods

Range: throughout

Stan's Notes: Also called Dogtooth Violet, Yellow Trout Lily is a member of the Lily family, not a violet ("Dogtooth" refers to the tooth shape of its underground bulb). The common name "Trout" comes from its mottled leaves, which resemble the coloring of a Brown Trout. One of the most common spring wildflowers found carpeting deciduous forest floors, the Yellow Trout Lily reproduces mostly by underground bulbs. It may take up to seven years for a plant to be mature enough to flower. Nearly identical to the White Trout Lily (pg. 239), except for the flower color.

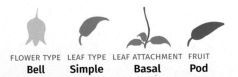

FLOWER TYPE
Bell

LEAF TYPE
Simple

LEAF ATTACHMENT
Basal

FRUIT
Pod

Partridge Pea
Chamaecrista fasciculata

Family: Pea or Bean (Fabaceae)

Height: 1–2' (30–60 cm)

Flower: a row of yellow flowers, each flower about 1–1½" (2.5–4 cm) wide, grows along the main stem at each leaf attachment; each flower is made up of 5 teardrop-shaped petals, 5 green pointed sepals and a dark red center (stamens); the 4 upper petals have a dark red base

Leaf: compound leaves, 2–3" (5–7.5 cm) long, attach alternately along the erect main stem; each leaf is made up of 20–30 oval leaflets, ½" (1 cm) long

Fruit: flat, thin, hairy pod-like container, similar to that of the common garden pea

Bloom: summer, fall

Cycle/Origin: annual, native

Habitat: dry, sun, prairies, sandy soils, along roads

Range: southern half of the L.P.

Stan's Notes: Partridge Pea is a common annual of native prairies throughout the southern half of the state. Does not have the characteristic pea flowers—resembles them only in that one petal is slightly larger than the other four and one of those is often curved. Its leaves fold up in direct sunlight, hence its other common name, Sensitive Pea.

FLOWER TYPE	LEAF TYPE	LEAF ATTACHMENT	FRUIT
Irregular	**Compound**	**Alternate**	**Pod**

Marsh Marigold
Caltha palustris

Family: Buttercup (Ranunculaceae)

Height: 1–2' (30–60 cm)

Flower: many round, green-and-yellow buds open to become 5–9 bright yellow petals (actually sepals), 1–1½" (2.5–4 cm) wide

Leaf: round, toothless basal leaves, 2–7" (5–18 cm) wide, with long stalks and a deep notch where the stalk attaches; upper leaves stalkless, on the stem (cauline), 1–2" (2.5–5 cm) wide

Bloom: spring

Cycle/Origin: perennial, native

Habitat: wet, sun, along ponds, streams, lakes

Range: throughout

Stan's Notes: Also called Cowslip, the Marsh Marigold is well known for its bright yellow flowers that bloom very early in the spring. This wildflower grows in or along quiet waterways, such as streams and ponds. The genus name, *Caltha*, comes from the Latin word for "cup," and describes the plant's upturned petal-like sepals that form a shallow cup. The common name "Marigold" comes from an Anglo-Saxon word meaning "marsh-gold." However, while the name is certainly a reasonable description of this plant, the Marsh Marigold is not a true marigold, but a type of buttercup. It is said the common name "Cowslip" comes from the fact that the plant grew on the hummocks and cows slipped on it when they went to the stream to drink.

FLOWER TYPE
Regular

LEAF TYPE
Simple

LEAF ATTACHMENT
Alternate

LEAF ATTACHMENT
Basal

Common Dandelion
Taraxacum officinale

Family: Aster (Asteraceae)

Height: 2–18" (5–45 cm)

Flower: what appears to be 1 large yellow flower, 1½" (4 cm), is actually a composite of many tiny flowers clustered together

Leaf: a rosette of simple basal leaves with deep lobes and sharp teeth

Bloom: spring, summer, fall

Cycle/Origin: perennial, non-native

Habitat: dry, sun, lawns, fields

Range: throughout

Stan's Notes: This non-native perennial is responsible for much water contamination, as people treat lawns with chemicals to eradicate it. In French, *dent-de-lion* refers to the teeth of its leaf edge, resembling the teeth of a lion. Its flowers open in the morning and close in the afternoon. Globe-like seed heads have soft hair-like bristles that resemble tiny parachutes to carry the seeds away on the wind. The Red-seeded Dandelion (not shown) is another species of dandelion in Michigan. Originally brought from Eurasia as a food crop, its leaves taste bitter but offer high vitamin and mineral content. Its long taproot can be roasted and ground for a coffee substitute.

FLOWER TYPE
Composite

LEAF TYPE
Simple Lobed

LEAF ATTACHMENT
Basal

Large-flowered Bellwort
Uvularia grandiflora

Family: Colchicum (Colchicaceae)

Height: 10–20" (25–50 cm)

Flower: drooping, pale yellow, bell flowers, 1–2" (2.5–5 cm) long, that appear to be weak and dehydrated; individual flowers have 6 petals

Leaf: long, pointed, lance-shaped, drooping leaves, 1–3" (2.5–7.5 cm) long; the stem passes through the base of the leaf as they alternate along the main stem

Bloom: spring

Cycle/Origin: perennial, native

Habitat: wet, shade, deciduous woods

Range: throughout

Stan's Notes: A single-stemmed plant that forks near the top into arching stems, the Large-flowered Bellwort has one to three drooping yellow flowers per stem. It grows in clumps containing up to several individual plants along horizontal underground roots (rhizomes), and its leaves have whitish downy hair underneath. The genus name *Uvularia* refers to this down-hanging flower's resemblance to the uvula. The Large-flowered Bellwort is one of only two species of bellwort in Michigan (six species grow in eastern North America). Wild Oats (pg. 351) looks similar but has a white flower. An attractive wildflower for a shade garden. When flowers are mature, they look wrinkled and droopy. After flowering, the stem lengthens and straightens.

FLOWER TYPE
Bell

LEAF TYPE
Simple

LEAF ATTACHMENT
Alternate

LEAF ATTACHMENT
Perfoliate

Sneezeweed
Helenium autumnale

Family: Aster (Asteraceae)

Height: 3–5' (90–150 cm)

Flower: each flower head, 1–2" (2.5–5 cm) wide, has 10–15 fan-shaped, bright yellow petals (ray flowers), each tipped with 3 lobes; yellow-green center (disk flowers) conspicuous, ball-like and protrudes above the petals; up to 100 flower heads per plant

Leaf: narrow, lance-shaped, stalkless leaves, ½–1" (1–2.5 cm) wide and 3–6" (7.5–15 cm) long, with widely spaced teeth; the edge of the leaf's base forms wings that extend down the main stem

Bloom: summer, fall

Cycle/Origin: perennial, native

Habitat: wet, sun, swamps, wet meadows and prairies, or along streams

Range: throughout

Stan's Notes: This plant often grows in a large dense clump and produces many flowers. Its ball-like disk flowers and unusually long leaf base edges (wings) help identify this member of the Aster family. Reportedly makes farm animals ill if eaten. Its dried leaves were once used as snuff and induced sneezing, giving rise to "Sneeze" in the common name. A similar species, Purple-headed Sneezeweed (*H. flexuosum*) (not shown), has a purplish brown flower center and is found in dry fields and prairies.

FLOWER TYPE **Composite**   LEAF TYPE **Simple**   LEAF ATTACHMENT **Alternate**

Thin-leaved Coneflower

Rudbeckia triloba

Family: Aster (Asteraceae)

Height: 2–5' (60–150 cm)

Flower: each plant is covered with 50–100 yellow flower heads, 1–2" (2.5–5 cm) wide, each flower is made up of 6–10 yellow petals (ray flowers) surrounding a brown cone-shaped center (disk flowers)

Leaf: lower leaves, 3–4" (7.5–10 cm) long, have 3 pointed lobes; upper leaves, 2–3" (5–7.5 cm) long, are simple and coarsely toothed

Bloom: fall

Cycle/Origin: annual or biennial, native

Habitat: dry, sun, fields, along roads, prairies

Range: southern half of the L.P.

Stan's Notes: Sometimes grown as a garden plant for its late autumn burst of color, Thin-leaved Coneflower can grow up to 100 flower heads per plant. Each petal (ray flower) is grooved along its length with a narrow notch at the tip. Look for the three-lobed lower leaves and simple upper leaves to help identify this wildflower, which looks like a miniature Black-eyed Susan (pg. 387).

FLOWER TYPE
Composite

LEAF TYPE
Simple

LEAF TYPE
Simple Lobed

LEAF ATTACHMENT
Alternate

Zigzag Goldenrod
Solidago flexicaulis

Family: Aster (Asteraceae)

Height: 1–3' (30–90 cm)

Flower: several round clusters, 1–2" (2.5–5 cm) wide, of yellow flower heads located at each of the leaf joints (axis); individual flowers, ¼" (.6 cm) wide, have only 3–4 petals (ray flowers)

Leaf: pointed, coarse-toothed, oval leaves, 1–3" (2.5–7.5 cm) long, alternate along the stem; leaves are dark green with a short leafstalk

Bloom: fall

Cycle/Origin: perennial, native

Habitat: dry, shade, in clearings and along the edges of deciduous woods

Range: throughout

Stan's Notes: Zigzag Goldenrod is a woodland goldenrod with one to three erect stems per plant. The stems bend back and forth between each leaf attachment, hence the common name, "Zigzag" (this characteristic is sometimes hard to see, and is most obvious between the upper leaves). One of the few goldenrods with flower clusters located at each leaf joint rather than spikes near the top of the plant. The only goldenrod to grow in the forest. A nice plant for the shady flower garden.

CLUSTER TYPE	FLOWER TYPE	LEAF TYPE	LEAF ATTACHMENT
Round	**Composite**	**Simple**	**Alternate**

Wood Betony
Pedicularis canadensis

Family: Broomrape (Orobanchaceae)

Height: 5–14" (12.5–36 cm)

Flower: spike cluster, 1–3" (2.5–7.5 cm) tall, of yellow tubular flowers; individual flowers, ¾" (2 cm) long, can be yellow, white or red, but are always arranged in a tight fuzzy cluster

Leaf: highly divided, fern-like, narrow leaves, 1–3" (2.5–7.5 cm) long, covered in fine white hairs

Bloom: spring, summer

Cycle/Origin: perennial, native

Habitat: dry, woods, prairies

Range: throughout

Stan's Notes: Sometimes called Lousewort, this native perennial spreads by short horizontal roots (rhizomes), often forming large patches. Flowers can be all yellow, all red or bicolored (yellow and red). There are about 40 species of wood betonies in North America. The hairy leaves are often reddish. Most leaves rise from the base of the plant (basal), but it also has several stem leaves (cauline). A partially parasitic plant, obtaining some nutrients from the roots of other plants. Its genus name *Pedicularis* means "of lice." Sometimes called Lousewort due to the erroneous belief that if livestock ate the plant, they would become infested with lice.

CLUSTER TYPE
Spike

FLOWER TYPE
Irregular

LEAF TYPE
Simple Lobed

LEAF ATTACHMENT
Alternate

LEAF ATTACHMENT
Basal

Goat's Beard
Tragopogon dubius

Family: Aster (Asteraceae)

Height: 1–3' (30–90 cm)

Flower: a single large, yellow, dandelion-like flower head, 2–2½" (5–6 cm) wide, of many petals (ray flowers) but no center disk flowers; its stalk is swollen just below the flower head

Leaf: simple, grass-like leaves, 12" (30 cm) long and just ½" (1 cm) wide, clasp the stem

Bloom: spring, summer

Cycle/Origin: biennial, non-native

Habitat: dry, sun, fields, along roads

Range: throughout

Stan's Notes: Sometimes called Yellow Goatsbeard, this European import looks like a large dandelion and is common along roads and in open fields. Its large yellow flower head, which turns to face the sun, opens only on sunny mornings and closes by noon, which has led to another common name, Johnny-go-to-bed-at-noon (several other plants share this moniker). Its long taproots can be dug and roasted as a coffee substitute, and the entire plant produces a sticky, milky sap. The seed head looks like a giant dandelion plume or like an old gray goat's beard, and children often call its mature flower heads "blow balls." Some people spray these seed heads with hairspray and use them in dried flower arrangements.

FLOWER TYPE
Composite

LEAF TYPE
Simple

LEAF ATTACHMENT
Alternate

LEAF ATTACHMENT
Clasping

Gray-headed Coneflower
Ratibida pinnata

Family: Aster (Asteraceae)

Height: 3–7' (90–210 cm)

Flower: up to 15 droopy yellow petals (ray flowers) surround a thimble-shaped cone (disk flower), 2–2½" (5–6 cm) tall, that is always taller than it is wide; 10–25 very showy flower heads per plant, each on an individual stalk

Leaf: highly divided leaves, up to 7" (18 cm) long, with many thin, coarsely toothed lobes; its basal leaves have long stalks up to 7" (18 cm) and its stalkless, undivided, upper leaves (cauline) become smaller near the top

Bloom: summer

Cycle/Origin: perennial, native

Habitat: dry, sun, along roads, prairies

Range: southern half of the L.P.

Stan's Notes: A magnificently tall plant of roadsides and native prairies, the Gray-headed Coneflower's tall, thin, hairy stems support striking yellow flowers with relaxed or droopy petals. After pollination, the cone (disk flower) dries to a light gray color and smells strongly of spice when crushed. Also called Yellow Coneflower.

FLOWER TYPE
Composite

LEAF TYPE
Simple Lobed

LEAF ATTACHMENT
Alternate

LEAF ATTACHMENT
Basal

Hoary Puccoon
Lithospermum canescens

Family: Borage (Boraginaceae)

Height: 6–12" (15–30 cm)

Flower: flat cluster, 2–3" (5–7.5 cm) wide, of orange-to-yellow flowers; individual flowers, ½" (1 cm) wide, have 5 petals that form a small tube at the base; flower stem is in shape of a question mark

Leaf: nearly stalkless, narrow, hairy leaves, ½–1" (1–2.5 cm) long, alternate along a hairy stem

Bloom: spring

Cycle/Origin: perennial, native

Habitat: dry, sun, rocky soils, prairies, along roads

Range: southern half of the L.P.

Stan's Notes: At least six species of *Lithospermum* in Michigan. Eighteen species of puccoon are found in North America. This plant usually grows with only one main stem topped with a cluster of flowers. The fine grayish hairs that cover its stems and leaves give it the "Hoary" name. "Puccoon" is a Native American name for any plant used for color dye (the roots of the puccoon make a red dye). This plant looks similar to orange Butterfly-weed (pg. 93), although it's not generally as tall or robust.

CLUSTER TYPE	FLOWER TYPE	LEAF TYPE	LEAF ATTACHMENT
Flat	**Regular**	**Simple**	**Alternate**

Winter Cress
Barbarea vulgaris

Family: Mustard (Brassicaceae)

Height: 1–2' (30–60 cm)

Flower: several spike clusters, 2–3" (5–7.5 cm) long, of bright yellow flowers; individual flowers, ¼" (.6 cm) wide, are made up of 4 petals that form a cross

Leaf: lower leaves have long stalks, 3–5" (7.5–12.5 cm), with up to 5 lobes, the end or terminal lobe being the largest; coarsely toothed, upper stem leaves (cauline) often clasp the stem

Fruit: thin, erect, pod-like containers split lengthwise into 2 curled sides to release many tiny black seeds

Bloom: spring, fall

Cycle/Origin: biennial, non-native

Habitat: wet, sun, open fields, along roads or railroad tracks

Range: throughout

Stan's Notes: Winter Cress is one of the first wildflowers to bloom each spring, often while snow remains on the ground, hence its common name (it also blooms again in late autumn). A favorite of deer, it is one of the first green "deer foods" in the spring. Its tiny black seeds are very hot and peppery, and have been used as a pepper substitute; the plant itself has been used as a poultice to treat wounds in folk medicine. A member of the Mustard family (but not a true mustard), Winter Cress has six stamens—four long and two short.

CLUSTER TYPE
Spike

FLOWER TYPE
Regular

LEAF TYPE
Simple Lobed

LEAF ATTACHMENT
Alternate

FRUIT
Pod

Black-eyed Susan
Rudbeckia hirta

Family: Aster (Asteraceae)

Height: 1–3' (30–90 cm)

Flower: large flower head, 2–3" (5–7.5 cm) wide, with a brown button-like center (disk flowers) surrounded by 10–20 daisy-like yellow petals (ray flowers); 1 to numerous flower heads per plant

Leaf: slender, toothless, very hairy leaves, 2–7" (5–18 cm) long; each leafstalk clasps a hairy stem; winged leafstalk

Bloom: summer, fall

Cycle/Origin: perennial or biennial, native

Habitat: prairies, fields, dry, open, deciduous woods

Range: throughout

Stan's Notes: Also called the Brown-eyed Susan, look for three prominent veins on each leaf and a characteristic winged leafstalk clasping each erect, straight stem. Originally a native prairie plant, it is now found in just about any habitat, including along roads and in disturbed fields. Its seeds make an abundant food source for Goldfinches and House Finches. The species name, *hirta*, Latin for "hairy" or "rough," refers to the plant's hairy nature. Who "Susan" was remains unknown. A host plant for the black-and-orange striped Silvery Checkerspot caterpillars. The caterpillars camouflage themselves with bits of the flower secured by silk while feeding on the brown centers of the Black-eyed Susan.

FLOWER TYPE **Composite**   LEAF TYPE **Simple**   LEAF ATTACHMENT **Alternate**   LEAF ATTACHMENT **Clasping**

Green-headed Coneflower
Rudbeckia laciniata

Family: Aster (Asteraceae)

Height: 5–8' (150–240 cm)

Flower: each plant grows 20–50 large composite flower heads; individual flower heads, 2–3" (5–7.5 cm) wide, have 8–10 drooping yellow petals (ray flowers) surrounding a cone-shaped green center (disk flowers)

Leaf: lower leaves, 5–8" (12.5–20 cm) long, have 3–5 sharp lobes and coarse teeth; upper leaves, 2–3" (5–7.5 cm) long, are simple, coarsely toothed and nearly clasp the stem

Bloom: summer

Cycle/Origin: perennial, native

Habitat: wet, sun, fields, ditches, prairies

Range: throughout

Stan's Notes: A tall, robust, prairie perennial, Green-headed Coneflower grows in moist soils throughout the state. Look for its green center (cone) and drooping yellow petals—along with the lobed lower leaves and simple upper leaves—to help identify. Often seen growing in ditches or along roads and near old homesteads, it is also called Golden Glow. A good plant for a butterfly garden. Its flowers attract Monarchs and Fritillaries to feed on nectar.

FLOWER TYPE
Composite

LEAF TYPE
Simple

LEAF TYPE
Simple Lobed

LEAF ATTACHMENT
Alternate

389

Yellow Lady's Slipper
Cypripedium parviflorum

Family: Orchid (Orchidaceae)

Height: 4–24" (10–60 cm)

Flower: 1–2 fragrant, muddy yellow flowers, 2–3" (5–7.5 cm) tall; a single large, inflated, yellow petal surrounded by 4 brownish purple (actually 2 petals and 2 petal-like sepals) twisted petals

Leaf: basal leaves, up to 8" (20 cm) long, with many deep parallel veins; smaller stem leaves (cauline) alternate and clasp the stem

Bloom: spring, summer

Cycle/Origin: perennial, native

Habitat: wet, shade, deciduous woods, swamps and bogs

Range: throughout

Stan's Notes: The genus name *Cypripedium* comes from "Cypris," the Latin name for the goddess Venus of Cyprus, and the Greek *pedilon*, meaning "sandal." Orchids are highly specialized plants needing their own special fungus growing on their roots to survive. This is why they are nearly impossible to transplant and should be enjoyed in the wild only. Orchid seeds are dust-like specks that consist only of an embryo and have no stored food. The seeds depend on being invaded by fungal filaments, called hyphae, to infuse them with nutrients. This process takes place over several years before any roots or shoots develop. All native orchids are protected by conservation laws in Michigan.

FLOWER TYPE **Irregular**   LEAF TYPE **Simple**   LEAF ATTACHMENT **Alternate**   LEAF ATTACHMENT **Basal**

Wild Parsnip
Pastinaca sativa

Family: Carrot (Apiaceae)

Height: 2–4' (60–120 cm)

Flower: 7–10 flat clusters, 2–3" (5–7.5 cm) wide, of many tiny yellow flowers, each only ¼" (.6 cm)

Leaf: compound leaf, 5–7" (12.5–18 cm) long, made up of 5–15 coarse-toothed, oval leaflets; its leafstalk has wide wings

Bloom: spring, summer

Cycle/Origin: biennial, non-native

Habitat: wet, sun, fields, roadsides

Range: throughout

Stan's Notes: Very common along wet roadsides and ditches, Wild Parsnip's many flowers often turn an entire roadside sunny yellow in the spring. A native of Eurasia, this biennial was introduced from Europe as a garden food crop. Its long taproot is too woody to be edible after the second year of growth. Now considered a weed in many places. Can cause photodermatitis if touched. After you touch the plant, skin will blister and weep when exposed to sunlight. Wear gloves and long sleeves and pants if you work among the plants. A host plant for the Black Swallowtail butterfly caterpillar.

CLUSTER TYPE
Flat

FLOWER TYPE
Regular

LEAF TYPE
Compound

LEAF ATTACHMENT
Alternate

False Sunflower
Heliopsis helianthoides

Family: Aster (Asteraceae)

Height: 3–4' (90–120 cm)

Flower: bright yellow flower heads, 2–3" (5–7.5 cm) wide, with 20–30 petals (ray flowers) with a yellow center (disk flowers); only one flower head per stem

Leaf: coarsely toothed, lance-shaped leaves, 1–3" (2.5–7.5 cm) long, with a very short leafstalk, which makes the leaf appear to be clasping a smooth stem

Bloom: summer

Cycle/Origin: perennial, native

Habitat: dry, sun, fields, prairies

Range: throughout

Stan's Notes: Also called Ox-eye, the False Sunflower can be found throughout the state. Unlike true sunflowers, both the ray and disk flowers of the False Sunflower produce fruits. All flowers are borne on a single stalk, which is usually smooth (although some are rough). Look for a slight swelling in the stem just below the flower to help identify this perennial. A nice butterfly garden plant that is hardy and easy to grow.

FLOWER TYPE   LEAF TYPE   LEAF ATTACHMENT
Composite   **Simple**   **Opposite**

Woodland Sunflower
Helianthus spp.

Family: Aster (Asteraceae)

Height: 3–7' (90–210 cm)

Flower: each plant produces 1–10 yellow flower heads, 2–4" (5–10 cm) wide, made up of 9–17 petals (ray flowers) that surround a yellow center (disk flowers)

Leaf: opposite, dark green, finely toothed, lance-shaped leaves, 3–8" (7.5–20 cm) long; leaves are rough to the touch and pale white underneath

Bloom: summer, fall

Cycle/Origin: perennial, native

Habitat: shade, edges and clearings of deciduous woods

Range: throughout

Stan's Notes: Flower heads of the Woodland Sunflower have yellow petals and a yellow center, and its stems and leaves are rough (but occasionally smooth) to touch. Its upper leaves nearly clasp the stem while lower leaves have short leaf stems, and the plant usually grows in large clumps, each plant leaning toward available sunlight. The genus name, *Helianthus*, comes from the Greek *helios* (sun) and *anthus* (flower). A great producer of seeds for sparrows and finches.

FLOWER TYPE
Composite

LEAF TYPE
Simple

LEAF ATTACHMENT
Opposite

Common Tansy
Tanacetum vulgare

Family: Aster (Asteraceae)

Height: 2–4' (60–120 cm)

Flower: several flat, 2–4" (5–10 cm) wide, clusters of yellow, button-like composite flower heads; individual flower heads, ½" (1 cm) wide, look like common daisy flower heads without the white petals

Leaf: deeply divided, fern-like leaves, 4–8" (10–20 cm) long, with many sharp teeth

Bloom: summer, fall

Cycle/Origin: perennial, non-native

Habitat: dry, sun, along roads, disturbed soils

Range: throughout

Stan's Notes: A tall plant of roadsides and old fields (and sometimes grown in gardens), Common Tansy often forms dense patches of bright yellow flowers. Its leaves have a strong bitter or medicinal odor. The plant has been used in many folk remedies, although usually with poor results because the plant contains a toxic oil called tanacetum. The highly fragrant leaves are sometimes used as a substitute for sage in scented bags and pillows. A native of Europe, it can now be found around the world. Its composite flowers are composed only of disk flowers and look like little flat buttons.

CLUSTER TYPE
Flat

FLOWER TYPE
Composite

LEAF TYPE
Simple Lobed

LEAF ATTACHMENT
Alternate

Yellow Flag Iris
Iris pseudacorus

Family: Iris (Iridaceae)

Height: 2–3' (60–90 cm)

Flower: 1 to several large, yellow flowers, 2½–4" (6–10 cm) wide, rising on tall stiff stalks; individual flower has 6 petals, which are actually 3 large, backward-curving, petal-like sepals and 3 smaller, narrow, upright petals

Leaf: long, narrow, sword-like blades, 1" (2.5 cm) wide and 8–32" (20–80 cm) long, similar to garden irises

Fruit: large, green, round-ended pod, 1½–2" (4–5 cm), containing multiple seeds

Bloom: spring, summer

Cycle/Origin: perennial, non-native

Habitat: wet, sun or shade, wetland edges, lakes and rivers

Range: widely scattered in the L.P., usually near cities

Stan's Notes: This European garden import now grows wild along water in clumps of tall, erect, sword-like leaves with many flowers. These clumps are created by toxic, horizontal underground roots (rhizome), which many cultures have used medicinally. Its largest petals are actually sepals. Insects pollinate by walking along the sepals, passing under the plant's male and female flower parts. The term "flag" from the Middle English *flagge*, means "rush" or "reed," and refers to the plant's leaves. "Iris" is derived from the Greek word for "rainbow," describing the wide range of flower color.

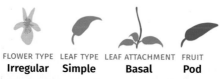

FLOWER TYPE
Irregular

LEAF TYPE
Simple

LEAF ATTACHMENT
Basal

FRUIT
Pod

Stiff Goldenrod
Solidago rigida

Family: Aster (Asteraceae)

Height: 1–5' (30–150 cm)

Flower: many small, yellow flower heads, ⅓" (.8 cm) wide, form a flat cluster, 3–4" (7.5–10 cm) wide; each individual flower head has 7–10 yellow petals (ray flowers) and 20–30 center disk flowers

Leaf: blade-like, stalked basal leaves, 10" (25 cm) long, are rough to the touch and stand erect; leaves on the stem (cauline) are round and fleshy, alternate and clasping

Bloom: summer, fall

Cycle/Origin: perennial, native

Habitat: dry, sun, fields, prairies, along roads

Range: throughout the L.P.

Stan's Notes: A common goldenrod of open fields and prairies, Stiff Goldenrod usually grows two or three stems that branch into flower heads near the top of the plant. Its main stem and leaves are hairy, making them rough to touch, and its basal leaves are stiff and stand erect, hence the common name. The plant's round fleshy leaves help to differentiate it from other species of goldenrod, making this goldenrod easier to identify. The flowers are an excellent source of nectar, attracting butterflies, bees, flower flies and beetles.

CLUSTER TYPE
Flat

FLOWER TYPE
Composite

LEAF TYPE
Simple

LEAF ATTACHMENT
Alternate

LEAF ATTACHMENT
Basal

LEAF ATTACHMENT
Clasping

Yellow Water Lily
Nuphar lutea

Family: Water Lily (Nymphaeaceae)

Height: aquatic

Flower: floating, cup-shaped, yellow flowers, 3–5" (7.5–12.5 cm) wide, made up of 4 large yellow (sometimes green) petals, surrounded by up to 3 small petal-like sepals; the flowers stand up to several inches above the water surface

Leaf: round or heart-shaped, deeply notched, toothless, shiny green floating leaves, 3–8" (7.5–20 cm) long

Bloom: summer, fall

Cycle/Origin: perennial, native

Habitat: small lakes, channels, bays

Range: throughout

Stan's Notes: Also called Bullhead Lily, the Yellow Water Lily is commonly found in small ponds, lakes and streams and is the only yellow pond lily in Michigan. This common pond lily requires quiet water because it is rooted to the lake or pond bottom. Its roots produce large rhizomes that are often eaten by muskrats and beavers. Stems and leaves have air channels that trap air to keep the plant afloat. Its flowers usually open only on sunny afternoons.

FLOWER TYPE
Regular

LEAF TYPE
Simple

LEAF ATTACHMENT
Basal

Common Sunflower
Helianthus annuus

Family: Aster (Asteraceae)

Height: 3–10' (90–300 cm)

Flower: sunny yellow flower heads, 3–6" (7.5–15 cm) wide, each with 15–20 yellow petals (ray flowers), surround a large dark brown or purple center (disk flower); each plant has 2–20 flowers

Leaf: stiff, coarse-toothed triangular or heart-shaped leaves, 3–7" (7.5–18 cm) long, alternate along a very coarse stem

Bloom: summer, fall

Cycle/Origin: annual, native

Habitat: dry, sun, fields, along roads, open places

Range: throughout

Stan's Notes: A smaller, wild version of the Giant Sunflower, which is often cultivated in gardens and fields. Unlike the giant variety, the wild Common Sunflower usually branches several times but still produces many nutritious seeds. Used for food by many people in history, the Common Sunflower's seeds can be used in the making of flour, oil, and even medicine. It is often seen growing along highways where the seeds of maturing plants are dispersed along the road by wind created from passing cars and trucks. Sunflowers do not follow the sun, as widely believed. Their heads face the morning sun once they mature and begin to bloom, thus most flowers face east.

FLOWER TYPE   LEAF TYPE   LEAF ATTACHMENT
Composite   **Simple**   **Alternate**

Butter-and-eggs
Linaria vulgaris

Family: Plantain (Plantaginaceae)

Height: 1–2' (30–60 cm)

Flower: a spike, 3–6" (7.5–15 cm) long, of irregular, yellow-and-orange pea-like flowers, 1" (2.5 cm) tall, each made of 5 petals fused together in a snapdragon-like flower; a thin spur below each flower contains nectar

Leaf: thin, pale, gray green, grass-like leaves, 1–2" (2.5–5 cm) long, sometimes set opposite near the base but alternate above

Bloom: spring, summer, fall

Cycle/Origin: perennial, non-native

Habitat: dry, sun, open fields, disturbed soils, along roads

Range: throughout

Stan's Notes: Introduced from Europe, Butter-and-eggs escaped from gardens and now grows throughout Michigan. A two-toned flower whose orange part, known as the "honey guide," acts like a target to guide insects into the long spur of the flower, ensuring that the insect pollinates it before getting the nectar. It often grows in patches, reproduces along a horizontal underground stem called a rhizome and is a favorite of the hummingbird-like Sphinx Moth. This plant takes its name from its yellow (butter) and orange (egg yolk) flowers. When its flower is pinched, it opens wide like a frog's mouth, providing its other common name, Toadflax.

CLUSTER TYPE **Spike** FLOWER TYPE **Irregular** LEAF TYPE **Simple** LEAF ATTACHMENT **Alternate**

Golden Alexanders

Zizia aurea

Family: Carrot (Apiaceae)

Height: 1–3' (30–90 cm)

Flower: tiny creamy yellow flowers, ¼" (.6 cm) wide, form flat clusters, 5–6" (12.5–15 cm) across

Leaf: a single (compound) leaf that divides into 3 stalks; each stalk with 3–7 narrow, coarse-toothed, pointed leaflets

Bloom: spring

Cycle/Origin: perennial, native

Habitat: wet, sun, ditches, along roads, moist fields, woods

Range: southern half of the L.P.

Stan's Notes: The Golden Alexanders is related to parsley and is part of the Carrot family, whose members share a similar flat-topped cluster of flowers (umbel). Its stems are often tinged with red. Commonly seen in large patches in late spring along roads in wet ditches, it is often confused with Wild Parsnip (pg. 393), which also has a flat-topped cluster of yellow flowers. It is also related to Water Hemlock (pg. 313), a deadly plant of the same habitat with a flat cluster of white flowers. Was once used to heal wounds, and relieve fevers and syphilis.

CLUSTER TYPE FLOWER TYPE
Flat   **Regular**

LEAF TYPE   LEAF ATTACHMENT
Twice Compound   **Alternate**

Canada Goldenrod
Solidago canadensis

Family: Aster (Asteraceae)

Height: 2–5' (60–150 cm)

Flower: a mass of small individual yellow flower heads, ¼" (.6 cm) wide, arranged in large, arching, spike clusters, 3–9" (7.5–22.5 cm) tall; the tip of the tallest flower cluster nods to one side

Leaf: narrow, up to 6" (15 cm) long, rough to touch, sharp teeth along edges; fewer leaves near base of stem

Bloom: summer, fall

Cycle/Origin: perennial, native

Habitat: dry, sun, open fields, prairies

Range: throughout

Stan's Notes: This common plant, often seen in roadside patches, reproduces by sending up new plants from roots (clones), creating patches 8–30' (2.4–9.1 m) wide, excluding other plants from the site. There are over 100 types of goldenrod in North America and over 20 in Michigan, all looking similar, thus difficult to identify. While most yellow autumn flowers are a type of goldenrod and are often mistakenly blamed for hay fever, only 1–2% of autumn airborne pollen is from goldenrod (most hay fever is caused by ragweed). Goldenrod is pollinated by insects, including beetles, ambush bugs, flies, midges and bees, which are attracted to the flower's abundant nectar. Goldenrod stems are often invaded by insect larvae (usually a solitary wasp or fly larvae), causing large swellings (galls).

CLUSTER TYPE	FLOWER TYPE	LEAF TYPE	LEAF ATTACHMENT
Spike	**Composite**	**Simple**	**Alternate**

Yellow Sweet Clover
Melilotus officinalis

Family: Pea or Bean (Fabaceae)

Height: 3–6' (90–180 cm)

Flower: spike clusters, 8" (20 cm) long, of irregular yellow flowers, ¼" (.6 cm) tall

Leaf: each leaf divides into 3 narrow, toothed lance-shaped leaflets, ½–1" (1–2.5 cm) long

Fruit: egg-shaped pod

Bloom: spring, summer, fall

Cycle/Origin: annual or biennial, non-native

Habitat: wet or dry, sun, along roads, open fields

Range: throughout

Stan's Notes: A non-native plant introduced from Europe via Eurasia, Yellow Sweet Clover was once grown as a hay crop, but has escaped and now grows throughout Michigan along roads and fields. This very fragrant plant smells like vanilla when its leaves or flowers are crushed. The genus name, *Melilotus*, is Greek for "honey," referring to its use as a nectar source for bees. Nearly identical to the White Sweet Clover (pg. 329), except for the flower color. It also blooms a couple of weeks earlier than White Sweet Clover. The rodenticide warfarin was developed from the chemical dicoumarol in sweet clover.

CLUSTER TYPE	FLOWER TYPE	LEAF TYPE	LEAF ATTACHMENT	FRUIT
Spike	**Irregular**	**Compound**	**Alternate**	**Pod**

Evening Primrose
Oenothera biennis

Family: Evening Primrose (Onagraceae)

Height: 2–5' (60–150 cm)

Flower: many pale yellow flowers, 1–2" (2.5–5 cm) tall, in a round cluster, 6–10" (15–25 cm) wide; individual flowers have 4 petals and an X-shaped center (stigma)

Leaf: narrow, lance-shaped leaves, 4–8" (10–20 cm) long, alternate along a hairy stem; leaves are rough to the touch and often tinged with red along the edge

Fruit: blunt-topped green pod-like container, ½–2" (1–5 cm) long, with lengthwise ridges

Bloom: summer, fall

Cycle/Origin: biennial, native

Habitat: dry, sun, prairies, along roads

Range: throughout

Stan's Notes: As a biennial, the Evening Primrose produces a low ring (rosette) of leaves in its first year, sending up a tall flower stalk in its second. Its flowers bloom starting at the bottom going up, opening a few at a time. The flowers open in the evening and last until about noon the next day before wilting, hence the common name. Its pods contain many seeds eaten by wildlife. A number of other species of Evening Primrose are found in Michigan and all but one have the unique X-shaped center (stigma) and yellow flowers. The flowers of this plant are pollinated by Sphinx Moths at night.

CLUSTER TYPE
Round

FLOWER TYPE
Regular

LEAF TYPE
Simple

LEAF ATTACHMENT
Alternate

FRUIT
Pod

flower

Common Mullein
Verbascum thapsus

Family: Snapdragon (Scrophulariaceae)

Height: 2–6' (60–180 cm)

Flower: a club-like spike 1–2' (30–60 cm) long; of many, small, yellow flowers, ¾–1" (2–2.5 cm) wide, packed along the stalk, each flower has 5 petals, and only a few open at a time, from the top down

Leaf: large basal leaves, 12–15" (30–37.5 cm) long, with thick covering of stiff hairs, velvety to touch; stalk-less upper leaves (cauline) clasp the main stem at alternate intervals, leaves progressively smaller toward top of stalk

Bloom: summer, fall

Cycle/Origin: biennial, non-native

Habitat: dry, sun, fields, along roads

Range: throughout

Stan's Notes: A European import, this plant is known for its very soft, flannel-like leaves, hence its other common name, Flannel Plant. This biennial takes two years to reach maturity. The first year it grows as a low rosette of large, soft leaves; in the second, a tall flower stalk sprouts. It's said the Romans dipped its dried flower stalks in animal tallow to use as torches. Victorian women rubbed the leaves on their cheeks, slightly irritating their skin, to add a dash of blush. Early settlers and Native Americans placed the soft woolly leaves in their footwear for warmth and comfort. Its dried stems stand well into winter.

CLUSTER TYPE	FLOWER TYPE	LEAF TYPE	LEAF ATTACHMENT	LEAF ATTACHMENT	LEAF ATTACHMENT
Spike	**Regular**	**Simple**	**Alternate**	**Basal**	**Clasping**

CHECKLIST/INDEX BY SPECIES

Use the boxes to check the flowers you've seen.

GLOSSARY

Alternate: A type of leaf attachment where the leaves are singly and alternately attached along the stem, not paired or in whorls.

Annual: A plant that germinates, flowers and sets seed during a single growing season and returns the following year only from seed.

Anther: A part of the male flower that contains the pollen.

Axil: The angle formed between a stem and a leafstalk.

Axis: A point on the main stem from which lateral branches arise.

Basal: Leaves at the base of a plant, near the ground, usually grouped in a round rosette.

Bell flower: A single downward-hanging flower with petals fused together that form a bell-like shape.

Berry: A fleshy fruit containing one or many seeds (e.g., a grape or tomato).

Biennial: A plant that lives for only two years, and blooms in the second year.

Bract: A leaf-like structure usually found at the base of a flower, often appearing as a petal.

Bulb: A short, round, underground shoot used as a food storage system, common in the Onion family.

Calyx: The name for the collective group of all of the sepals of a flower.

Cauline: Leaves that attach to the stem distinctly above the ground, as opposed to basal leaves that attach near the ground.

Clasping: A type of leaf attachment where the leaf base partly surrounds the plant's main stem at the point of attachment; the leaf grasps the stem without a leafstalk.

Cluster: A group or collection of flowers or leaves.

Composite flower: A collection of tiny flowers that appear as one large flower. Usually made up of ray and disk flowers, pertaining to members of the Aster family (e.g., common daisy).

Compound leaf: A single leaf composed of a central stalk and two or more leaflets.

Coniferous: Plants that do not shed their leaves each autumn (e.g., pine and spruce).

Corm: A short, thickened, vertical, underground stem used to store food.

Deciduous: Plants that shed their leaves each autumn (e.g., maples and oaks).

Disk flower: The small tubular flowers in the central part of a composite flower in the Aster family, such as the center of a daisy.

Ephemeral: Lasting for only a short time each spring.

Flat cluster: A group of flowers that form a flat-topped structure, which enables insects to easily land and thereby complete pollination; exhibited by plants of the Carrot family (e.g., Queen Anne's Lace).

Gland: A tiny structure, usually secreting oil or nectar, sometimes found on leaves, stems, stalks and flowers, such as in Gumweed.

Irregular flower: A flower that does not have the typical round shape, usually made up of 5 or more petals that are fused together in an irregular shape (e.g., pea or bean flower).

Leaflet: One of many leaf-like parts of a compound leaf. A compound leaf is made up of two or more leaflets.

Lip: The projection of a flower petal, or the "odd" petal, such as the large inflated petal of an orchid; may also refer to the lobes of a petal.

Lobed: A simple leaf with one or more indentations (sinuses) along its edge that do not reach the center or base of the leaf, (e.g., dandelion or oak leaf).

Margin: The edge of a leaf.

Mycorrhiza: A mutually beneficial relationship between a fungus and the root system of a plant.

Node: The place or point of origin on a stem where leaves attach (or have been attached).

Opposite leaves: A type of leaf attachment where the leaves are situated directly across the stem from each other.

Palmate: A type of compound leaf where three or more leaflets arise from a common central point which is at the end of a leafstalk, such as in Wild Lupine.

Parasitic: A plant or fungus that derives its food or water chiefly from another plant, to the detriment of the host plant.

Perennial: A plant that lives from several to many seasons, returning each year from its roots.

Perfoliate: A type of leaf attachment where the base of a leaf is connected around the main stem so that the stem appears to pass through the stalkless leaf (e.g., Boneset).

Petal: A basic flower part, usually brightly colored, serving to attract pollinating insects.

Pistil: The female part of a flower made up of an ovary, style and stigma, often in the center of a flower.

Pod: A dry fruit that contains many seeds (e.g., a pea pod).

Pollination: The transfer of pollen from the male anther to the female stigma, resulting in the production of seeds.

Ray flowers: One of many individual outer flowers of a composite flower in the Aster family (e.g., a single petal of a daisy flower).

Regular flower: A flower with 3–20 typical petals arranged in a circle.

Rhizome: A creeping, underground, horizontal stem.

Rosette: A cluster of leaves arranged in a circle, often at the base of the plant, as in Common Mullein.

Round cluster: A group of many flowers that form a round structure, giving the appearance of one large flower.

Saprophytic: A plant or fungus that lives on dead organic (plant) matter, neither parasitic nor making its own food (e.g., Indian Pipe).

Seed head: A group or cluster of seeds.

Sepal: A member of the outermost set of petals of a flower, typically green or leafy but often colored and resembling a petal (e.g., lily).

Sheath: A tubular leaf-like structure that surrounds the stem (e.g., Spotted Coralroot).

Simple leaf: A single leaf with an undivided or unlobed edge.

Spadix: A highly specialized, thickened spike with many small flowers that are crowded together (e.g., Jack-in-the-pulpit). See spathe.

Spathe: A large, usually solitary, petal-like bract often enclosing a group of flowers, such as a spadix (e.g., Jack-in-the-pulpit). See spadix.

Spike cluster: Many flowers on a single spike-like stem, giving the appearance of one large flower.

Spur: A hollow, tube-like appendage of a flower, usually where nectar is located (e.g., Jewelweed).

Stamen: Collectively, the male parts of a flower consisting of an anther and filament.

Stem leaf: Any leaf that is found along a plant's stem, as opposed to a leaf at the base of a plant (basal). See cauline.

Stigma: The female part of the flower that receives the pollen.

Stipules: A pair of basal appendages of a leaf, not attached to the leaf blade.

Stolon: A creeping stem on the surface of ground (e.g., Creeping Charlie).

Toothed: The jagged or serrated edge of a leaf, resembling the teeth of a saw.

Tube flower: Similar to a bell flower with fused petals that form a tube, usually turned upward, not hanging downward.

Whorled: A circle or ring of three or more similar leaves, stems or flowers originating from a common point.

Wing: A flat extension at the base of a leaf or edge of a leafstalk, sometimes extending down the stem of the plant.

Woody: Stems that are hard and brown, usually with bark; not a soft green stem.

NOTES

NOTES

NOTES

ABOUT THE AUTHOR

Naturalist, wildlife photographer and writer Stan Tekiela is the originator of the popular state-specific field guide series that includes *Birds of Michigan Field Guide*. Stan has authored more than 190 educational books, including field guides, quick guides, nature books, children's books, playing cards and more, presenting many species of animals and plants.

With a Bachelor of Science degree in Natural History from the University of Minnesota and as an active professional naturalist for more than 30 years, Stan studies and photographs wildlife throughout the United States and Canada. He has received various national and regional awards for his books and photographs. Also a well-known columnist and radio personality, his syndicated column appears in more than 25 newspapers, and his wildlife programs are broadcast on a number of Midwest radio stations. Stan can be followed on Facebook and Twitter. He can be contacted via www.naturesmart.com.

OTES